Library of
Davidson College

# A WAR OF INFORMATION

*The Conflict Between Public and Private U.S. Foreign Policy on El Salvador, 1979–1992*

Michael R. Little

UNIVERSITY
PRESS OF
AMERICA

Lanham • New York • London

Copyright © 1994 by
**University Press of America,® Inc.**
4720 Boston Way
Lanham, Maryland 20706

3 Henrietta Street
London WC2E 8LU England

All rights reserved
Printed in the United States of America
British Cataloging in Publication Information Available

### Library of Congress Cataloging-in-Publication Data
Little, Michael R.
A war of information : the conflict between public and private U.S. foreign policy on El Salvador, 1979–1992 / Michael R. Little.
p.   cm.
Includes bibliographical references and index.
1. United States—Foreign relations—El Salvador.   2. El Salvador—Foreign relations—United States.   I. Title.
E183.8.S2L58      1993      327.7307284—dc20      93–31781 CIP

ISBN 0–8191–9311–9 (cloth : alk. paper)

The paper used in this publication meets the minimum requirements of American National Standard for Information Sciences—Permanence of Paper for Printed Library Materials, ANSI Z39.48–1984.

# Contents

| | |
|---|---|
| **Preface** | vii |
| **Acknowledgements** | xi |
| **Introduction** | xiii |
| **Chapter 1  The Background to U.S. Policy** | 1 |
| Idealism versus Realism | 1 |
| Balance of Power | 3 |
| Imperialism or Status Quo? | 4 |
| Historical Context | 5 |
| Grenada | 7 |
| Somoza and the Sandinistas | 7 |
| Reflexive anti-Americans | 9 |
| Notes | 9 |
| **Chapter 2  The Rise of the FMLN** | 15 |
| Evolution and Organization of the FMLN/FDR | 17 |
| Unification | 18 |
| Military Structure | 19 |
| The Vietnamese Connection | 23 |
| The Sandinistas | 23 |
| FMLN Strategy | 24 |

Notes

**Chapter 3  El Salvador and the Cold War**  33

    The 1979 Coup  35
    No More Cubas  36
    Treaty Obligations  41
    Reagan Policy  42
    Notes  46

**Chapter 4  Private Foreign Policy**  51

    Revolutionary Policy  51
    Principled Realism  53
    An Attitude as Much as a Policy  56
    Notes  57

**Chapter 5  Organizations Opposing U.S. Policy**  59

    Committee in Solidarity with the People of El Salvador  60
    Movement Characteristics  61
    Case Study: Omaha Central America Response Team  63
    Responsibility  65
    'Peace' Cults  66
    Accountability  68
    Double Standards  68
    Reform versus Revolution  70
    Notes

**Chapter 6  War of Information**  77

    Propaganda  77
    Demonstrations  78
    Disinformation: The School of the Americas  81
    Disinformation: Soviet Bloc Support for the FMLN  82
    Disinformation: The Death Toll  88

Indoctrination as Entertainment
The Coffee Boycott 95
Notes 99

**Chapter 7   Private Intervention** 109

Fundraising 110
War Industry 113
The Repopulation Program 114
'Internationalist' Mercenaries 117
The Six Jesuits 119
Notes 119

**Chapter 8   The FMLN: Terrorists or Guerrillas?** 125

Assassination and the 'War of the Mayors' 126
Death Squads for Democracy 127
The Zona Rosa Massacre 128
Fundraising 130
Economic Disruption 132
Mine Warfare 133
Terrorists or Freedom Fighters? 135
Notes 135

**Chapter 9   Did CISPES Believe in Human Rights?** 141

Notes 144

**Chapter 10   The Media and Congress** 147

The 1989 FMLN Offensive in the News 147
Congress 149
Ronald Dellums (D-CA) 152
Patricia Schroeder (D-CO) 153
Notes 154

**Chapter 11   The FBI Investigation** 157

The Armed Resistance Unit and CISPES 158

v

| | |
|---|---|
| The Congressional Inquisition into the FBI Investigation of CISPES | 161 |
| Liberal Coverup? | 164 |
| Notes | 169 |

**Chapter 12   The End of the War**                    173

| | |
|---|---|
| Peace Settlement | 174 |
| After the War | 175 |
| Notes | 177 |

**Conclusion**                                          179

**Appendix**                                            181

**Selected Bibliography**                               183

**Index**                                               187

# Preface

During the 1980s the United States was at war in Central America. Although Nicaragua seems to have attracted the most attention, the actual center appears to have been El Salvador, with complementary campaigns in Nicaragua and Honduras, and spillover into Costa Rica. The war in Guatemala is of such long standing and different character that it may be regarded as something separate, although there were certainly connections with what was going on to its southeast. The war was undeclared - at least by the United States - but was real nonetheless, especially for those directly involved. The methods, means, and motivation for fighting it have been rendered obscure by a fog of misinformation and half-truths generated by the participants and their supporters. This book is an attempt to at least partly clear the air on one aspect of the war; the battle over policy.

People have a tendency to regard the problems of others as somehow more tractable than their own. This tendency appears to have underlain (and undermined) official United States policy for combatting guerrillas in both Vietnam and Central America. In both cases an attempt to coopt the 'revolution' through agrarian and other reform was essential to the U.S. program, without heed to idea that such reform was scarcely less an imposition on the government and people of a sovereign, foreign country than the insurgency it was meant to counter.

On a global level this temptation to meddle (and belief that it might actually work) seems to be magnified when the other people happen to live in a small, remote country. El Salvador is geographically closer than, for example, Europe, but perceptually it is much more remote. It sometimes seems as if the whole Central American isthmus has existed all these years in some sort of stasis, spasmodically animated by U.S. attention. It is easy to imagine it frozen in time - caudillos in brass trimmed khaki uniforms, quaint Spanish colonial cities, jungles and mountains, coffee and bananas, peasants clearing land with their machetes frozen aloft in blurred mid-swing - until some newsworthy catastrophe occurs and history is thus free to proceed.

This perception is unfortunate for two reasons. First, it is a grave injustice to a collection of nations and people with a colorful, interesting past, who have made and are making their own contributions to world civilization and culture. Second, it opens the door to fringe groups with an agenda to shape - some would say to warp - what perceptions do reach the U.S. public; perceptions which, due to the inordinate influence of domestic politics on foreign relations, tend to drive U.S. policy. This is clearly what happened during the 1980s.

In the case of El Salvador the United States government was not the only entity to succumb to the illusion that someone else's problems could be solved from afar. The opposition to official U.S. policy took the form of the radical leftist minority in the U.S. picking out a militant political minority in El Salvador, bestowing on it the title of "the People of El Salvador," and backing it in its attempt to violently remake Salvadoran society into a form more in tune with its own ideology. Ironically, this deliberate intervention in internal Salvadoran politics was often justified in the name of 'non-intervention;' one of many ironies, hypocrisies, and outright deceptions of this movement.

There were parallels between the Vietnam War and the war in El Salvador. (For one thing, many of the people who had helped save Southeast Asia from democracy tried to do the same thing for El Salvador.) But the same can be said of many other conflicts. Actually, when examining the leftist involvement in Central America, the Spanish Civil War comes to mind. In Spain in the 1930s and in Central America in the 1980s, the left elevated a local conflict with ideological overtones into a war between good and evil, and trooped off to do their 'internationalist' duty. "No Pasaran!" was the cry before Madrid and Managua. Leftist guerrillas were lionized. *The*

*Nation* reported, editorialized and agonized. And the vast bulk of the American population didn't seem to pay much attention.

There was some effect, however. As in Spain in the 1930s, left-leaning celebrities ostentatiously cast their lot with the visibly Marxist movements in the region. The U.S. news media clearly favored the left, and films and novels about the conflict tended to present the party line. Considering the alienated pose of the cultural and media elite, this was to be expected. However, the adoption of the Sandinista and FMLN cause by liberal Democrats in the United States Congress came as something of a surprise. If this support had remained a matter of criticism and debate, it would have remained within the democratic tradition. But it didn't. Members of the United States Congress actually involved themselves with support networks for declared enemies of the United States, and used their positions to protect these organizations from official investigation, even while the networks were conducting clearly criminal activities.

One would think that with Iran-Contra being beaten to death and conspiracy theories abounding, there would be some interest in investigating such a grotesque breach of faith. But with the continued ascendancy of the Democratic party in Congress and the recent election of a Democratic President, it seems unlikely that any official investigation of liberal Democrat support of left-wing terrorist organizations will be tolerated. Considering the example of the Vietnam War and the activities of such luminaries as Jane Fonda, it is even less likely that anyone in Congress will be prosecuted for it. Any such implication of leftist political misbehavior provokes a parrot cry of "McCarthyism! McCarthyism!" among the liberal elite. There is a time element involved, in that most of the events occurred in the 1980s, which may as well be ancient history. Add to this the acknowledged leftward tilt of the national news media, and it becomes doubtful that any clear picture of how well the FMLN and its allies succeeded in Congress will be forthcoming in the immediate future.

Unless, of course, people outside these systems look into it. The sections of this book devoted to the matter barely scratch the surface of the material available. It is to be hoped that others may find such study rewarding.

# Acknowledgements

All photos in this book are courtesy of the Embassy of El Salvador, whose personnel (and those of the consulate in San Francisco) were most courteous and helpful, but, due to their official positions, cannot be acknowledged by name. They have my heartfelt thanks, anyway. Among the people who can be named, the original impetus for this work came from Professor John Rasmussen of California State University at Stanislaus, for whom it was written as a seminar paper. Dr. Terry Karl, at Stanford, suggested sources for the more coherent 'counterpolicy' and provided information on the 1991 Salvadoran elections. Professor H. Carl Camp of the University of Nebraska at Omaha kindly reviewed the manuscript and suggested changes, some of which determined its final form. Simon Henshaw, at the Central America desk of the U.S. State Department, provided some key documents, including the official study prepared by the U.S. Embassy on the death toll in El Salvador.

Cynthia Arnson of Americas Watch was an alternative source of casualty information. The Omaha Central America Response Team (OCART) allowed me to examine their collection of network literature. Michael Shuman of the Institute for Policy Studies provided an excellent package of Sister City material. Many others took the time to answer questions (sometimes rather impertinent ones) and/or mail information about their programs.

J. Michael Waller's book on the FMLN support networks, *The Third Current of Revolution*, was useful as a secondary source and its bibliography was superb. The staff of *Soldier of Fortune* magazine, especially Alex McColl, answered questions and suggested sources of firsthand information. One of those sources, Mr. Greg Walker, provided insight on the U.S. advisory effort and helped me obtain Dr. Benjamin Schwartz's critique of U.S. policy.

Special acknowledgement must go to Jan Knippers Black. In her appendix titled "Professional Ethics in the Study of Latin America" to *Latin America, Its Problems and Its Promise*, she stated: "Honesty - not neutrality - is the guiding principle of scholarship."

# Introduction

U.S. government policy towards El Salvador was developed in the context of East-West conflict, specifically to prevent a Marxist - and so presumably pro-Soviet - movement from taking over El Salvador. Aspects of this policy as it evolved included promotion of political reform as the primary weapon against the guerrillas, bolstered by economic aid - both to repair the damage wrought by sabotage and war, and to promote economic growth - and shielded by the armed forces.[1] From the beginning this policy was opposed by segments of U.S. society, who achieved a remarkable degree of organization and through that became effective opponents of U.S. policy, and thus (intentionally or not) effective allies of the insurgents.

Their role in the war in El Salvador became particularly important after the middle 1980's, when the increasing effectiveness of the Salvadoran armed forces in the field and the decline of the rebels' perceived political legitimacy apparently forced a shift in the FMLN's strategy:

> The shift was away from the government's military force to the source of that force's power - the aid provided by the United States. As a result, borrowing heavily on the training and instruction received from the Vietnamese, the strategy became one of taking a relatively low profile militarily, negotiating, targeting the U.S. Congress as the principle objective in the war of information, and waiting for the United States to disengage from Central America and the Salvadoran conflict.[2]

There was a conflict between official U.S. policy in El Salvador and the agenda - essentially a "private foreign policy" - of these groups. As evident from the quotation above this conflict was another, integral aspect of the war in El Salvador. As such it deserves attention as a relatively neglected aspect of low intensity conflict; the use of domestic sympathizers by a foreign enemy to support that enemy's war effort. This book will examine the background to the official policy and discuss its relation to the situation in El Salvador and the private organizations opposing it.

### Notes

1. Viron Vaky, "Reagan's Central American Policy: An Isthmus Restored," *Central America - Anatomy of Conflict*, ed. Robert S. Leiken (New York: Pergamon Press, 1984), 235.

Enrique Baloyra-Herp, "The Persistent Conflict in El Salvador," *Current History*, March 1991, 121-122.

Jose Z. Garcia, "Tragedy in El Salvador," *Current History*, January 1990, 40.

2. Max G. Manwaring and Court Prisk, *El Salvador at War*, with a preface by Ambassador Edwin G. Corr (Washington, D.C.: National Defense University Press, 1988), 411.

Chapter 1

# The Background to U.S. Policy

It is often asserted that U.S. foreign policy during the 1980s was guided by 'Realism,' as opposed to the fuzzy-minded or laudable (depending on the observer's orientation) 'Idealism' of the Carter administration. To evaluate this fairly requires a look at what these terms actually mean. One of the leading theorists of 'realism' in international relations was Hans Morgenthau.

**Idealism versus Realism**

Hans Morgenthau, in his book *Politics Among Nations*, contrasted two schools of modern political thought. "One believes that a rational and moral political order, derived from universally valid abstract principles, can be achieved here and now." This school "assumes the essential goodness and infinite malleability of human nature," and asserts that failure is not caused by the theory, but comes from "lack of knowledge and understanding, obsolescent social institutions, or the depravity of certain isolated individuals or groups." Often the programs advanced by members of this school include liquidation of such problems as a prerequisite for success. This is "idealism," one form of which is "legalism-moralism," in which "standards of thought appropriate to other spheres" are imposed upon politics.[1] The human rights focus of the Carter foreign policy is often cited as an example of legalism-moralism.[2]

> The other school believes that the world, imperfect as it is from a rational point of view, is the result of forces inherent in human nature. To improve the world one must work with those forces, not against them. This being inherently a world of opposing interests and of conflict among them, moral principles can never be fully realized, but must at best be approximated through the ever temporary balancing of interests and the ever precarious settlement of conflicts. This school, then, sees in a system of checks and balances a universal principle for all pluralist societies. It appeals to historic precedent rather than to abstract principles, and aims at the realization of the lesser evil rather than of the absolute good.[3]

This, then, is "realism." The Reagan policy, which developed in an atmosphere publicly critical of the Carter policy, is usually presented as conforming to realism. In fact it appears that neither policy was purely one nor the other, and both tended to blur together on many important points. In an almost existential twist, realism became something of an ideal for U.S. policymakers, and one which they didn't always live up to. The two primary causes for this deviation are closely linked; the definition of 'national interest' and the problem of 'balance of power.'

The term national interest has been borrowed and redefined to fit the ideology of groups with little or no connection with realism. According to Morgenthau, however, national interest is defined as power, and the policy maker's primary and overriding concern should always be how an issue or course of action will affect the nation's power.[4] The pursuit of power is seen as the driving force of international relations.[5]

There are two brakes on this struggle for power. One is the balance of power, while the other consists of "normative limitations . . . in the form of international law, international morality, and world public opinion."[6] Those concerned with U.S. policy around the turn of the decade came to see these normative limitations as completely ineffective in influencing Soviet behavior.[7] They decided that the balance of power between the Soviet Union and the United States was the only effective brake on aggressive Soviet expansionism, and this perception was the chief motivating force behind U.S. involvement in El Salvador.

**Balance of Power**

The traditional form of the balance of power is multipolar, but the rise of the two superpowers in the post-WWII era made it bipolar; an arrangement Morganthau considered unstable. A further destabilizing factor was the "principle means" used to "maintain or re-establish the balance of power," which was armaments.[8] In this unstable situation precariously balanced by the potential - real or perceived - for violence, it was to be expected that reactions to perceived threats would tend to err in the safest direction; paradoxically, toward extreme self-protection.

To ameliorate this unstable balance of power and to make a realistic foreign policy work properly, Morganthau proposed a "revival" of diplomacy, operating under nine rules. The first four he termed "fundamental."

1. Diplomacy must be disvested of the crusading spirit.

2. The objectives of foreign policy must be defined in terms of the national interest and must be supported with adequate power.

3. Diplomacy must look at the political scene from the point of view of other nations.

4. Nations must be willing to compromise on all issues that are not vital to them.[9]

Compromise is, of course, anathema to the idealist, but necessary for the smooth functioning of human society on virtually any scale. Morgenthau identified five prerequisites for diplomatic compromise.

1. Give up the shadow of worthless rights for the substance of real advantage.

2. Never put yourself in a position from which you cannot retreat without losing face and from which you cannot advance without grave risks.

3. Never allow a weak ally to make decisions for you.

4. The armed forces are the instruments of foreign policy, not its master.

5. The government is the leader of public opinion, not its slave.[10]

As will be seen, due to their own brand of idealism the Reagan administration policymakers violated most of Morgenthau's rules of diplomacy and compromise, and deviated significantly from pure 'realism' in their approach to Central American policy. Although the resultant approach was more nationalistic than the Carter policy, it cannot accurately be described as 'imperialistic,' as its more strident critics have charged.[11]

**Imperialism or Status Quo?**

According to Morgenthau "It is widely believed that whatever a nation, such as Great Britain, China, the Soviet Union, or the United States, does in order to maintain its preponderant position in certain regions is imperialistic."[12] The FMLN and its sycophants followed this line, and could be expected to condemn virtually anything the U.S. did as imperialistic.[13] However, this is not so much the result of Marxism as it is of phobic anti-Americanism. "Those who are opposed on principle to a particular nation and its policies, such as Anglophobes, Russophobes, and anti-Americans, regard the very existence of the object of their phobia as a threat to the world."[14] Thus they could be expected to apply "imperialism" - as a fuzzily defined revolutionary pejorative - to U.S. policy.

In fact U.S. policy was not aimed at conquest, but at preventing further Soviet penetration in the Americas, and thus keeping current power relations more or less intact. It was a classic application of the Monroe Doctrine.[15] "The manifestation of the policy of status quo which has had the greatest importance for the United States and has been the cornerstone of its foreign relations is the Monroe Doctrine."[16]

It thus seems evident that the U.S. Central American policy, far from being aggressively imperialistic, was actually defensive in nature. The right to national defense is largely taken for granted, but much bewilderment has been expressed as to how involvement in a tiny country's civil war served to defend the United States. A look at the historical context makes the picture somewhat clearer, and the changes in policy more comprehensible.

**Historical Context**

The mid-1970's were a bleak time for U.S. foreign policy. The Southeast Asian dominoes all tumbled in 1975; Cambodia to the Khmer Rouge on April 17, South Vietnam to the North on April 30, and Laos to the Pathet Lao on December 3.[17]

Angola received its independence from Portugal on November 11, which event was, by that time, just another footnote in an ongoing civil war. The three independence movements had already turned from fighting the Portuguese to fighting one another. One of the three local factions, the Popular Movement for the Liberation of Angola (MPLA), was supported by Fidel Castro and heavily supplemented in the field by Cuban troops.[18]

> He [Castro] had trained MPLA guerrilla officers in Cuba, and when the internal power struggle erupted, he quietly dispatched 250 Cuban combat advisers in May 1975 to organize MPLA forces. ... Late in September and early in October, three Cuban freighters delivered military detachments and arms to Angola and, belatedly, Soviet arms began arriving through Brazzaville. In early October there were about 1,500 Cuban Army personnel in Angola. On October 23, South Africans in force entered Angola in Operation Zulu, and Cuba responded with a troop

airlift in "Operation Carlota." ... In February 1976, Castro had fifteen thousand troops in Angola ... .[19]

With this Soviet and Cuban support the MPLA gained control of the major cities and came to be regarded as the legitimate government. Another part of Africa where Cuban and Soviet forces were used to help a Marxist regime was Ethiopia. The Emperor Haile Selassie, long supported by the United States, was deposed on September 12, 1974, and died August 27, 1975. The junta which deposed him organized a ruling council, later called the Derg, headed by Brigadier Teferi Benti. On February 3, 1977 Benti was in turn overthrown and killed by a Communist faction under Lieutenant Colonel Mengistu Haile Mariam. Since human rights violations provoked a cutoff of U.S. aid on February 24th, in May the new government requested military assistance from the USSR and Cuba. The response was massive, as evidenced by the April 7, 1979 Ethiopian offensive against the Western Somali Liberation Front in the Ogaden Desert. This offensive was commanded by Soviet General Vasily Petrov and 17,000 Cuban troops were employed alongside 60,000 Ethiopians.[20]

In Iran a U.S. ally, the Shah Mohammad Reza Pahlavi, was deposed and left the country on January 16, 1979. Adding insult to injury, the U.S. Embassy was seized and its personnel taken hostage November 4th.[21]

One of the few bright spots of the 1970's had been improving relations with the Soviet Union. However, by late in the decade it was becoming apparent that each side interpreted 'detente,' a 'lessening of tensions,' differently.

> "International detente," an idea promoted by the Soviet Union as one manifestation of peaceful coexistence, was understood in the United States to mean something other than what it meant to the U.S.S.R. There is no simple answer to why that happened. George F. Kennan wrote that he had never "entirely understood why an impression got about that there was beginning, in our relationship with the Soviet Union, a new period of normalization and relaxation of tensions, to be sharply distinguished from all that had gone before." ... The Kremlin welcomed a certain amount of cooperation, on its terms, but it never accepted the idea of abandoning competition, either military or ideological. One of the great fallacies of detente was the idea that if the So-

viet Union were engaged in economic, trade, cultural, and other agreements, the West would be able to moderate the Soviets' voracious appetite for expansion and promote a shift in the U.S.S.R.'s global aims. Nothing could be further from reality. . . .[22]

On December 27, 1979 the U.S.S.R. invaded Afghanistan during a coup, which it had engineered to install a more sycophantically pro-Soviet dictator.[23] Detente died. As if awakened from a pleasant dream by a dash of cold water, the U.S. looked around at a world dropped jarringly back into the Cold War framework. It appeared that the Reds had the initiative in a worldwide wave of conquest. Iran was an oddity, but suspicion was that a Soviet connection would appear in time. And suddenly Communist weeds were sprouting in our own 'back yard.'[24]

**Grenada**

On March 13, 1979, Maurice Bishop of the New Jewel Movement (NJM) overthrew Sir Eric Gairy, the eccentric Prime Minister of Grenada.[25] Gairy was absent lobbying Kurt Waldheim for a United Nations conference on Unidentified Flying Objects. Despite Bishop's anointing himself as the "people's leader" and the NJM presenting itself as the true "party of the people," at the time the NJM only had forty-five full members.[26] Bishop had also provoked a certain amount of suspicion two years earlier by a comment he made during an interview by *Bohemia*, a magazine printed in Cuba.

> The triumph of socialism in our country will only be possible through firm ties with the socialist world and close cooperation with the more advanced governments of the region.[27]

The 'socialist world' was generally interpreted (by both the East and West) at the time to mean the Soviet bloc. Thus the shock of the "first coup d'etat in modern times in the English-speaking Caribbean" was compounded with a certain foreboding when the new government established diplomatic relations with Cuba on April 14.[28]

## Somoza and the Sandinistas

Nicaragua sees itself as a nation of poets, and there is a kind of poetic justice to the fall of the Somoza dynasty. The founder of that dynasty came to power through one of those typical situations where *norteamericano* idealism collided with Central American political reality. As part of a U.S. attempt to bring democracy to Nicaragua, the Nicaraguan Army (notoriously a power base for coups) was disbanded and replaced by an 'apolitical' National Guard (that is, one that was neither Liberal nor Conservative), headed by a clever young man who spoke excellent English; Anastasio Somoza. After six years of fighting to bring stability and democracy to Nicaragua, the U.S. Marines left on 1 January, 1933. On 2 February the same year the democratically elected government of Dr. Juan Sacasa managed to make peace with the rebels led by Augusto Cesar Sandino - the original Sandinistas. On 21 February the next year Somoza had Sandino and his immediate circle taken out and shot.[29]

This incident reveals a central misperception by the U.S. about Central America. The real problem was never Liberal versus Conservative, it was *caudillismo* - caudillo versus caudillo. Thus, instead of solving the problem, creating an armed, 'apolitical' body simply made a new caudillo out of whomever said body owed its allegiance to. And since all connection had been deliberately severed with the nation's political parties, that allegiance could only go to its commanding officer, Somoza. The result was a country turned into something like a feudal estate, a "ranch" as Frank McNeil termed it.[30]

Forty-five years later his son, Anastasio Somoza Debayle, was deposed by a popular uprising in which a new set of Sandinistas played a prominent - but more visible than substantial - part. Having alienated most of the population through gross corruption and violence, Somoza was forced to flee on July 17, 1979. As the largest, best armed and best organized political body left in Nicaragua, the Sandinistas quickly stepped into the resultant power vacuum. They were not able to have Somoza taken out and shot, but while he was in exile in Asuncion, Paraguay, a sympathetic (at least) terrorist group - the Argentine Peoples' Revolutionary Army (ERP - 'Montoneros') - blew up his Mercedes with an anti-tank rocket on September 17, 1980, which approaches the same thing.[31]

With Somoza out of the way a broad-based National Reconstruction Government was formed. Almost immediately the Sandinistas began to marginalize and edge out the non-Sandinistas, until what had started out as a fairly representative body became the Sandinista Directorate.[32]

> The victory of the armed struggle, made possible by Cuban help and American diplomatic reticence, guaranteed that the new rulers of Nicaragua would not have to keep the promises of democracy and non-alignment made in extremis, but instead would try to consolidate the revolution along Leninist lines and place the country in the Soviet camp.[33]

As usual, Nicaragua had exchanged one dictatorship for another. The only thing really different in this case was that one warlord had been traded for a committee of warlords.

**Reflexive anti-Americans**

Important from the U.S. standpoint was the Sandinista 'knee-jerk' anti-U.S. orientation. Apologists for the Sandinistas have charged that they were driven to it by the U.S. government. Actually, anti-Americanism filled a similar role in Sandinista ideology as anti-Semitism did in that of the Nazis. It was embedded in their thinking from the beginning, as evident in their Program of 1969, and despite a certain amount of deceptively soothing rhetoric it was never excised.[34]

- Their organization was named for a man whose chief accomplishment was fighting the 1927-1933 U.S. occupation of Nicaragua. A textbook from the Sandinista 1980 literacy campaign contained the following sentences: "Sandino fought the Yankees. The Yankees will forever be defeated in our motherland."[35]
- Their Marxist-Leninist orientation made them reflexively 'anti-imperialist,' with the U.S. identified as the chief 'imperialist' power in the world.
- Fidel Castro was their idol, model, and mentor. According to Frank McNeil, the Sandinistas could never have won without Cuban

material and training aid, which started well before their rise to power in 1979.[36] Castro's sentiments with regard to the U.S. are well known.

- Their anthem contains the lines "We will fight the Yankee, For he is the enemy of humanity," and did so even while they were soaking up millions of dollars in U.S. aid.[37]

Thus, operating on the theory that 'the enemy of my enemy must be my friend,' it is no surprise that they willingly jumped into the arms of the Soviet Union.[38] A whole new set of dominoes was being set up. And one of the wobbliest was El Salvador.

## Notes

1. Hans Morganthau, *Politics Among Nations*, 6th Ed. (New York: Alfred A. Knopf, 1985), 3.

2. Jeane Kirkpatrick, "U.S. Security and Latin America," *The Central American Crisis Reader*, ed. Robert S. Leiken & Barry Rubin (New York: Summit Books, 1987), 509-514.
   The problem with the Carter policy was not so much its focus on human rights, but the lack of definition of precisely what "human rights" meant, and the perception that this focus was at the expense of U.S. global interests.

3. Morganthau, 14.
   "Realism" has often been condemned as amoral. Actually, as is evident from the quotation, moral principles do play a role in a realistic foreign policy, but are not the primary focus. Similarly, the Reagan policy was condemned as "illegal and immoral" by its opponents. As will be shown, it was neither.

4. Morganthau, 3.

5. Morganthau, 5.

6. Morganthau, 243.

7. Jean-Francois Revel, *How Democracies Perish* (New York: Harper & Row, 1983), 303-304.
   This may also be inferred by the failure of SALT II ratification process.

8. Morganthau, 200.

9. Morganthau, 584-588.

10. Morganthau, 588-591.

11. Joaquin Villalobos, "A Democratic Revolution For El Salvador," *Foreign Policy* 74 (Spring 1989): 109.

12. Morganthau, 59.

13. Miguel Castellanos, *The Commandante Speaks: Memoirs of an El Salvadoran Guerrilla Leader*, ed. Courtney Prisk (Boulder, Colorado: Westview Press, 1991), 100.

14. Morganthau, 59.

15. In this context "The Monroe Doctrine" should be taken in its most general form.

16. Morganthau, 55.

17. *The World Almanac 1991*, ed. Mark S. Hoffman (New York: Pharos Books, 1990); 694, 727 & 767.

18. Tad Szulc, *FIDEL: A Critical Portrait* (New York: Avon Books, 1986), 708-709.

19. Szulc, 709.

20. Otto von Pivka, *Armies of the Middle East* (New York: Mayflower Books, 1979), 97 & 163.

21. *The World Almanac 1991*, 719.

22. Arkady N. Shevchenko, *Breaking With Moscow* (New York: Ballantine Books, 1985), 379 - 380.

23. John Fullerton, *The Soviet Occupation of Afghanistan* (London: Methuan London, 1984), 36.

24. Jeane Kirkpatrick, "Dictatorships and Double Standards," *El Salvador: Central America in the New Cold War*, ed. Marvin E. Gettleman, Patrick Lacefield, Louis Menashe, David Mermelstein and Ronald Radosh (New York: Grove Press, 1982), 18.

25. JEWEL stood for Joint Endeavor for Welfare, Education and Liberation. It was founded in 1970 by Unison Whiteman. The NJM was created on March 11, 1973 when JEWEL merged with the Movement for Assemblies of the People (MAP).

26. Hugh O'Shaughnessy, *Grenada: Revolution, Invasion and Aftermath* (London: Sphere Books, 1984), 77.

27. United States Department of State, *Lessons of Grenada* (Washington, D.C.: Government Printing Office, 1986), 6.

28. O'Shaughnessy, 77.

29. Ivan Musicant, *The Banana Wars* (New York: MacMillan Publishing Company, 1990); 306, 359-361.

30. Frank McNeil, *War and Peace in Central America* (New York: Charles Scribner's Sons, 1988), 108.

31. Arturo Cruz, Jr., *Memoirs of a Counterrevolutionary* (New York: Doubleday, 1989), 123.

Cruz asserts that the Sandinistas were "too smart" to have any direct connection with the killing, but there are some oddities which point to some sort of role. Put simply, why would an Argentine guerrilla group, virtually exterminated in its own country, undertake the hazardous assassination of a Nicaraguan ex-dictator in Paraguay?

Martin Aristogui, "The Case of the Danish Assassin," *National Review*, 24 May 1993, 49.

Recent revelations by former ERP leader Jorge Ricardo Massetti point to the ERP hit team having done so on direct orders from the Sandinistas, who used the ERP for a number of such 'plausibly deniable' operations.

32. Cruz, 90-91.

33. McNeil, 113.

34. Sandinist Front of National Liberation (FSLN), "The FSLN Program of 1969," *The Central American Crisis Reader*, ed. Robert S. Leiken & Barry Rubin (New York: Summit Books, 1987), 148-153.

35. "The Literacy Campaign Textbooks (August 1980)," *The Central American Crisis Reader*, 235.

36. McNeil, 112.

37. "The Literacy Campaign Textbooks (August 1980)," *The Central American Crisis Reader*, 235.

38. Cruz; 97, 102 & 106.

According to Cruz, Eden Pastora arrived in Managua two days after the other leading Sandinistas. By the time he got to "El Chipote" (later in the month but before the 26th) "he found that Cuban advisors were in place" in the Sandinista command post. Cruz also speaks of a KGB officer attached to the Soviet Embassy in Washington who expressed surprise at how "rabidly pro-Soviet the Sandinistas were."

**Chapter 2**

# The Rise of the FMLN

The roots of the Salvadoran civil war are deeply embedded in 8Salvadoran culture, history and society. Two elements of the Latin tradition which are particularly important in understanding the conflict are 1) the authoritarian, hierarchal nature of traditional society, with clear class lines, and 2) the role of land ownership in helping define that class structure.[1]

Traditionally there were two classes in society; a propertied elite and a mass of smallholders and landless peasantry. The upper class saw their position as something of a right, in much the same spirit as the divine right of kings, and viewed their position atop the social pyramid as being in the natural order of things. They were the rightful stewards of the land, and best equipped to use it properly. To a certain degree the peasantry agreed with them, and accepted their place in society without serious question. There was in this arrangement, in its ideal form, a sense of mutual obligation between patron and peon.[2]

What upset this traditional stability in El Salvador was the move, in the last quarter of the 19th century, toward the development of large latifundias (plantations) growing cash crops such as coffee for the international market. Initially, to get the large tracts of land necessary for these latifundias, tenant farmers and sharecroppers were evicted. When still more land was needed, developers turned toward campesino smallholdings and village communal lands.[3] Even when a fair price was paid the money soon ran out, and most peasants found themselves as seasonal laborers, considerably worse off than they had been.[4]

In some respects this can be compared with the Enclosure Movement in England, which led to large scale urban migration, emigration, and unrest. Similar situations in other Latin American countries led (or at least contributed) to outright revolts, such as the 1910 Mexican Revolution, and El Salvador was no exception.[5] In the late 1920s - early 1930s a movement of the displaced and economically disadvantaged, their situation aggravated by the Depression, coalesced. The Salvadoran Communist Party attempted to organize this movement into an actual rebellion, but fumbled. The dictatorship of General Maximiliano Hernandez Martinez crushed the revolt, leading to such harsh actions as La Matanza in 1932 during which 10,000 to 30,000 Salvadoran peasants were massacred.[6] Augustin Farabundo Marti, a Communist with probable Trotskyite leanings and a leader of the rebellion, was among those arrested and shot.[7]

The landed elite (sometimes called the '14 Families') continued to be the most influential segment of Salvadoran society. The peasants' anger over inequitable land distribution and La Matanza was suppressed, but not wiped out. Increased urbanization, at least partly due to rural-urban migration by displaced campesinos, continued strain the traditional structure of Salvadoran society. As education and communication improved, rising social awareness and expectations prompted many Salvadorans to question their place and to speak out about perceived inequities. The rigid, hierarchal social structure allowed few outlets for such dissent, which was often met with disproportionate violence. This tended to radicalize dissidents and force them farther left, underground or into exile.[8] Ultimately, it drove some into contact with the only support structure for such movements; the Marxist revolutionary network which began to develop in Latin America during the 1960s, with revolutionary Cuba as a model and focal point.[9]

## Evolution and Organization of the FMLN/FDR

Charles Clements, in his book *Witness to War*, characterized the FMLN as 'Marxist' but inferred that actual Communists made up a tiny, not particularly influential proportion of the organization.[10] This characterization is disingenuous at best. In fact, all the factions which later united to form the FMLN/FDR had roots in the Salvadoran Communist Party (PCES).[11]

**FPL** - In 1970 Cayetanio Carpio, the secretary-general of a PCES front called the National Democratic Union (UDN), formed the militant Forces of Popular Liberation (FPL). Its primary political front was the Popular Revolutionary Bloc (BPR, or simply *El Bloque*), which was founded in 1975.[12]

**ERP** - In 1971-1972 the People's Revolutionary Army (ERP) was formed by members of the Young Communists, plus radical Christian Democrats and assorted hangers-on. The February 28 Popular League (LP-28) was its 'mass' organization, founded in 1977 but virtually disintegrated by the early 1980's. To replace it the Popular Workers' League (LPO) was organized in the late 1980s.

**FARN/RN** - The ERP fragmented in 1975 due to the 'trial' and execution of Roque Dalton by Joaquin Villalobos, resulting in the National Resistance Party (RN) being formed by Dalton's followers. Its guerrilla branch was called the Armed Forces of National Resistance (FARN). In 1976 the RN allied itself with the United Popular Action Front (FAPU), consisting primarily of radical Catholic reformers (followers of 'liberation theology'), which became its primary front group.

**FAL** - In 1979 the official Communist Party of El Salvador (PCES) formed the Armed Forces of Liberation (FAL). Its political front organization was the aforementioned UDN. Clements identified this group as the only Communist unit, apparently on the premise that the PCES was the 'official' Moscow-line party.

**PRTC** - A final ingredient of this leftist alphabet soup is the Revolutionary Party of Central American Workers (PRTC), which also formed in 1979. The Popular Liberation Movement (MPL) was its designated 'popular' organization, formed in 1980.

**Unification**

In January, 1980, three of the guerrilla groups, the FPL, ERP and FARN, joined to form the Unified Revolutionary Directorate (DRU). Later in the year the PRTC joined as well. Fidel Castro, as a condition for his support, ordered that all Salvadoran guerrilla organizations must come under unified command, so with the addition of the FAL the Farabundo Marti National Liberation Front (FMLN) was formed in October, 1980, with the Democratic Revolutionary Front (FDR) as its political branch.[13] There is a possibly apocryphal story that Fidel had the leaders of the various Salvadoran factions swear unity with hands together on an M-16 rifle, but true or not the story elegantly illustrates the origin of the FMLN/FDR and its relationship with Castro.[14]

On the political front, in 1979 the UDN joined several other organizations to form the Revolutionary Coordination of the Masses (CRM), or *Coordinadora*. The CRM became the political coordination committee between the various political fronts (BPR, FAPU, UDN, MLP and LP-28/LPO) and the Unified Revolutionary Directorate (DRU). The DRU also controlled such organizations as the Confederation of Cooperative Organizations of El Salvador (COACES), the National Association of Salvadoran Educators (ANDES), the National Unity of Salvadoran Workers (UNTS, "a leftist labor umbrella group composed almost entirely of FMLN-connected unions") and other 'unions.'[15] It received direction from both the FMLN and FDR. The FDR's primary 'legitimate' political front was the Democratic Convergence (CD), which participated in the political process and even criticized guerrilla excesses on occasion - points of friction between the FMLN's military leadership and the FDR hierarchy.[16]

## Military Structure

In general the FMLN's component tendencies had three types of combat units. These were 'regular' or 'main force' guerrilla units, urban 'commandos,' and local militia. These units were organized along the same lines as that suggested in Guevara's *Guerrilla Warfare*, except that officer titles seem to have been less formalized. The FAL, FARN and the PRTC each fielded one battalion of guerrillas apiece, while the FPL and ERP had brigades. Early in the 1980s the FMLN was credited with having 10,000 or so combatants, but total manpower circa 1988 was 7500, divided as follows:[17]

FPL - 3000 Combatants

Units:

Felipe Pena Mendoza Brigade (or Battalion Group)
Farabundo Marti Brigades - urban
Urban commandos
Militia

ERP - 2800 Combatants

Units:

Rafael Arce Zablah Brigade (BRAZ) - elite
Special force commandos
Urban terrorist cells
Strategic mobile guerrilla units
Militia

FAL - 450 Combatants

Units:

Rafael Aguinada Carranza Battalion
Revolutionary Action Groups (GAR) - urban commando

FARN - 900 Combatants

**Figure 1.** *FMLN 'regular' guerrillas - possibly ERP - circa 1990. Note Soviet-made SA-16 and (at least 4) East German MPiKMS-72s.*

Units:

Carlos Arias Battalion
Urban commandos

PRTC - 350 Combatants

Units:

Luis Adalberto Diaz Battalion
Urban Guerrillas - Mardoqueno Cruz June 21

Generally, 80% or so of the 'regular' guerrillas were out of the country at any given time, mostly in refugee camps in Honduras.[18] Similarly, the command, control and communications (C3) network was based in Nicaragua.[19] Within El Salvador, the military structure was based on 'fronts,' as follows:[20]

Metropolitan (San Salvador) Front - All

Feliciano Ana Western Front - FPL

Modesto Ramirez Central Front - FARN, PRTC

Anastacio Aquino Paracental Front - FPL, ERP, FAL

Francisco Sanchez Eastern Front - ERP, FARN, FAL, PRTC

Actual areas under occupation by the FMLN ('liberated zones') included isolated pockets, such as the area around the Guazapa volcano, and two small 'sanctuaries,' or *bolsones*. One was in eastern Chalatenango and northern Cabanas, while the other extended across northern Morazan and La Union. Both of these bolsones overlapped the border well into Honduras, and on that side included a number of UN-operated refugee camps.[21]

## The Vietnamese Connection

Besides Cuba the FMLN had very close relations with Vietnam. It saw the Vietnam War as a model to be followed, sent members

**Figure 2.** *FMLN militia members were usually older or younger than main force combatants.*

there to be trained (both in combat and politico-military skills), and received equipment (much of it ex-U.S.) from that source. Much of the FMLN's strategy appears to have been derived from Vietnam's experience, and it is here that the most striking parallels with the Southeast Asian conflict appear.

Miguel Castellanos traveled to Vietnam in September 1983 one of sixteen FMLN leadership trainees. The courses taught by the Vietnamese "emphasized the War of Information and concluded with the subjects of fighting imperialism (by taking the fight to the U.S. Congress) and negotiations - from which you take everything, give nothing, and use the time to consolidate gains."[22]

> They [the Vietnamese] explained that in all of the mobilization that took place in the United States, they were involved in a large way. Of course, they had the support of the socialist bloc, because they do have one thing; when the socialist bloc supports a movement on all sides, it is constant, especially at the political level. That's what happened in the United States. In other words, it was total war, total in the integral sense, a war at the political-military and diplomatic levels.[23]

## The Sandinistas

Another ally was the Sandinista regime in Nicaragua. This alliance was forged while the FSLN was still a guerrilla group and the various insurgent factions in El Salvador had yet to unite into the FMLN. After coming to power in Nicaragua the Sandinistas publicly denied any material involvement in the Salvadoran civil war and were often embarrassed by the FMLN's revelations (deliberate and accidental) to the contrary. The FMLN seems to have seen them as a close but inconstant ally due to the Sandinistas' preoccupation with consolidating their own revolution, which led them to cut off the arms flow to El Salvador from time to time.[24]

In 1987 Daniel Ortega admitted that arms might be going to the FMLN from Nicaragua, but conditioned this statement with the exculpatory explanation that if so, individual members of the party and not the party itself were doing it.[25] A more blatant setup for 'plausible denial' would be hard to find, which appears to have been prompted by provisions of the 1987 Esquipilas Accords calling for an end to support for insurgent movements such as the Nicaraguan Resistance and the FMLN.

Upon signing the accords the Salvadoran government lodged a complaint of massive Sandinista assistance to the FMLN. According to this complaint, the General Command of the FMLN was located in a military installation near Managua called 32-22 House. A logistics base was south of Managua near Kilometer 10 1/2, while training of FMLN guerrillas was accomplished by the EPS 30-11 Battalion and at Estero Caballo, near Realejo on the northwestern coast. A propaganda center operated in 'downtown' Managua, in an earthquake-damaged building described as "half-crumbled."[26]

Conclusive proof of Sandinista involvement in El Salvador surfaced three years later. Two Salvadoran Air Force aircraft were downed in late 1990 by Soviet-made SA-14 missiles. One launch tube was recovered, and a Soviet investigation determined that its serial number matched that of a missile sold to Nicaragua in 1986. Faced with this violation, not only of the Esquipilas accords but also of the terms of the weapons purchase from the USSR (which forbade transfer to third parties without permission), the Sandinistas denied it, denounced it as Yankee propaganda, then about-faced and arrested several lower-ranking EPS personnel to face charges.[27]

Besides material support the Sandinistas were very influential in the FMLN's strategic thinking. The FSLN's apparent success in 1979 provided a model for the 'insurrectionist' tendencies in the FMLN, but many of the lessons appear to have been misinterpreted.

**FMLN Strategy**

Carl von Clausewitz's observations on the relationship between war and politics is often paraphrased. In his book *On War* Clausewitz said that "War is not merely a political act, but also a real political instrument, a continuation of political commerce, a carrying out of the same by other means. . . ."[28] Nowhere is this more obvious than in revolutionary war, in which the revolutionaries openly intend to sweep aside one political system and replace it with another. And as the development of the FMLN's strategy to prosecute their war shows, the difference between actions ostensibly military and ostensibly political blurred. 'Military' action, such as terrorist attacks, was used to influence politics, and 'political' action was used to influence military capabilities, specifically by attempting to force a cutoff of U.S. military aid.

On May 10, 1975, Roque Dalton was executed, officially for "treason" but actually for "not accepting the militarist line" of Joaquin Villalobos' *foquista* clique within the ERP.[29] Besides illustrating the guerrillas' tendency to resolve internal squabbles with violence, this marks a turning point in the history of Salvadoran insurgent strategy. Until then the example of the Cuban Revolution, and the 'foco' theory of revolutionary war derived from it, were the primary influences on Salvadoran revolutionary strategy. 'Foco' theory held that military action was the most important facet of the struggle, and that political organization would spring more or less spontaneously from it. What organizations were to be put together under 'foco' were primarily to support the guerrillas in the field, and propaganda was to be derived from guerrilla victories.[30] However, what had worked in Cuba in the late 1950s didn't seem to do very well elsewhere.

By the mid 1970s both the rural foco and the urban terrorist movements had been defeated and discredited. The inadequacies of Guevara's and Debray's interpretations of the Cuban revolution were all too clearly revealed. . . .[A]ction took precedence over planning. The establishment of a sound political infrastructure was seen to be irrelevant, thus it was ignored. In retrospect this oversight proved, quite literally, to be fatal. . . . Since most insurgent movements lack the strength and support necessary for a complete and decisive military victory, they must - and in successful cases do - direct their efforts toward a political conquest. This can only be accomplished by integrating all economic, political, and military resources into a coherent, singular functioning unit.[31]

That at least one of the "tendencies" of what was to become the FMLN grasped these principles is seen by a statement released by the FPL in 1978. Having rejected the Moscow-line official Communist Party as too "bourgeois," this splinter group, led by Cayetanio Carpio, called for a more active program against the status quo using a Maoist "protracted war" strategy.

This breakup crystallized in March 1970 with the loss of senior leaders of those organizations (Salvadoran Communist Party, Salvadoran Communist Youth, unions, etc.) and the direction of new truly revolutionary organization that would propel the people's struggle in all fields - pacifist and violent, legal and illegal - having as its axis the revolutionary armed struggle within the framework of a prolonged people's revolutionary war strategy.[32]

The FPL went on to explain what it meant by "the people's struggle in all fields" with its "STRATEGIC TASKS IN THE REVOLUTIONARY PROCESS TOWARD THE ACHIEVEMENT OF A POPULAR SOCIALIST REVOLUTION." One of these tasks was to "Combine the armed struggle with other struggle tactics (legal, illegal, peaceful, violent, etc.) as tactical and strategic measures toward the development of a people's war."[33] Clearly, the FPL recognized that its war aims could be advanced by other types of political action than armed combat. They were probably influenced in this regard by Vietnamese revolutionary theory, but the basic concept, that of using less overtly violent political tactics for a military victory, is present in Western military science as well. To quote von Clausewitz:

> But now we come upon a peculiar means of influencing the probability of the result without destroying the enemy's Army, namely, upon the expeditions which have a direct connexion with political views. If there are any enterprises which are particularly likely to break up the enemy's alliances or make them inoperative, to gain new alliances for ourselves, to raise political powers in our own favor, etc., etc., then it is easy to conceive how much these may increase the probability of success, and become a shorter way towards our object than the routing of the enemy's forces.[34]

Thus the emphasis given to development of political fronts to support the guerrillas. Dalton's views were not precisely "people's protracted war," but there was a point of congruence in that he saw the need for political organization to support and complement military action. The FPL's exploitation of Dalton's status as a 'martyr' and emphasis on this point of congruence appears to have led the other groups to accept, at least overtly, this facet of the FPL's strategy.[35] This led to the development of political fronts not only in El Salvador, but in the United States, since such international support was another one of the "Strategic Tasks" from the FPL document: "Promote solidarity with all the peoples fighting imperialism and capitalism . . ." Paired with a similar statement promoting solidarity with Central American organizations, this signals an intent to actively cultivate foreign support. Considering the whole point of the "Strategic Tasks" program, it appears equally obvious that these "solidarity" organizations were to be integrated into the FPL's "people's war," as part of the "other struggle tactics (legal, illegal, peaceful, violent, etc.)."[36]

Among these sympathetic "peoples" was the radical left movement in the United States, which also had the advantage of being in a good position - both physical and political - to act as part of the war effort. Later developments show that the FMLN and the its U.S. allies - whatever their public statements[37] - came to see that "[t]he solidarity group itself was defined ultimately as another actor in the war, and the United States as another front, no more and no less . . .", to quote CISPES national staff member Van Gosse.[38]

Besides the use of the political weapon, another feature of "prolonged popular war" is duration, the idea of a small force defeating a larger one by wearing it down over time. Although the strategy is usually thought of as being Maoist in derivation,[39] this basic concept appears in *On War*.

> If then the negative purpose, that is the concentration of all the means into a state of pure resistance, affords a superiority in the contest, and if this advantage is sufficient to balance whatever superiority in numbers the adversary may have, then the mere duration of the contest will suffice gradually to bring the loss of force on the part of the adversary to a point at which the political object can no longer be an equivalent, a point at which, therefore, he must give up the contest. We see then that this class of means, the wearing out of the enemy, includes the great number of cases in which the weaker resists the stronger.[40]

Although Clausewitz was writing of weaker and stronger nations, the applicability of this idea to guerrilla warfare is obvious. But it must be noted that in the case of the FMLN, this aspect of the program was advocated by the FPL alone at first, and appears to have been more or less forced onto the other tendencies by events.

> ... inside the FMLN were organizations that have a short-term mentality, congenital to their political-ideological development, and they believed the arguments and the flattery of the Sandinistas, who believe in insurrectionalism. [sic] The FPL is more in tune with the theory of a prolonged popular war, in which each opportunity, each offensive, means a step forward in the process ... The ERP, the PRTC, and the RN believe that opportunities are decisive, ... blending the Cuban and Sandinista positions. [The failed 1982 'Final Offensive'] was an abortion arranged by the short-termers and the Cuban-Sandinistas.[41]

So the stage was set for a protracted civil war. The government of El Salvador and its allies - especially the United States - were on one side, and the FMLN and its allies, including the U.S.-based FMLN support network, were on the other.

## Notes

1. William W. Pierson and Federico G. Gil, *Governments of Latin America* (New York: McGraw-Hill, 1957), 60-62.

2. Pierson & Gil, 378-379.

3. Dr. Paul B. Goodwin, Jr., *Global Studies: Latin America*, 5th Ed. (Guilford CT: Dushkin Publishing Group, 1992), 28.

4. Walter LaFeber, *Inevitable Revolutions* (New York: W.W. Norton & Co., 1984), 73.

5. Fred R. Harris, "Mexico: Historical Foundation," *Latin America, Its Problems and Its Promise*, ed. Jan Knippers Black (Boulder CO: Westview Press, 1991), 288-289.

6. Richard Millett, "Central America: Background to the Crisis," *Latin America, Its Problems and Its Promise*, 323.

7. LaFeber, 73.

8. Millett, 328-330.

9. Yonah Alexander and Richard Kucinski, "The International Terrorist Network," *Latin American Insurgencies*, ed. Georges Fauriol (Washington DC: Government Printing Office, 1985), 48-49.

10. Charles Clements, M.D., *Witness To War* (New York: Bantam Books, 1984), 148.

11. Miguel Castellanos, *The Commandante Speaks: Memoirs of an El Salvadoran Guerrilla Leader*, ed. Courtney Prisk (Boulder, Colorado: Westview Press, 1991), Appendix A.
   There has been a consistent effort by FMLN supporters to discredit Castellanos, on the basis of his being a defector and a 'traitor.' That the FMLN itself considered him dangerously credible is evidenced by their taking the trouble to assassinate him.

12. Information on this group and the rest of the FMLN's constituent organizations was abstracted from several sources:
   Castellanos, 133-135.

Robert S. Leiken, "The Salvadoran Left," *Central America - Anatomy of a Conflict* (Elmsford NY: Pergamon Press, 1984), 115-117.

Che Guevara, *Guerrilla Warfare*, with an introduction and case studies by Loveman and Davies (New York: Monthly Review Press, 1961; repr. Lincoln NE: University of Nebraska Press, 1985), 408-409.

Max G. Manwaring and Court Prisk, *El Salvador At War: An Oral History* (Washington DC: National Defense University Press, 1988), 79-84.

Michael Radu & Vladimir Tismaneanu, *Latin American Revolutionaries: Groups, Goals, Methods*, (Washington DC: Pergamon-Brassey's, 1990), Chapter 15.

13. Brian Loveman and Thomas M. Davies, Jr., "El Salvador" case study, Che Guevara, *Guerrilla Warfare*, with an introduction and case studies by Loveman and Davies (New York: Monthly Review Press, 1961; repr. Lincoln NE: University of Nebraska Press, 1985), 408-409.

14. Raymond Bonner, *Weakness and Deceit* (New York: Times Books, 1984), 96.

15. House Subcommittee on Civil and Constitutional Rights, *Break-ins at Sanctuary Churches and Organizations Opposed to Administration Policy in Central America*, 100-42 (Washington DC: Government Printing Office, 1988), 29.

Many organizations, although ostensibly connected with the "unified" FMLN\FDR, had closer relations with component groups than with the umbrella organization as a whole. As two examples, ANDES was closely connected with the FPL/BPR, to which it was giving 50% of its foreign donations in 1984. The UNTS leadership was strongly influenced by the PCES, but was 'officially' under the DRU.

16. Castellanos, 105.

17. This information was abstracted from the following sources:
Castellanos, 133-135.
Robert S. Leiken, "The Salvadoran Left," *Central America - Anatomy of a Conflict* (Elmsford NY: Pergamon Press, 1984), 115-117.
Loveman and Davies, 408-409.
Manwaring and Prisk, 79-84.
Radu and Tismaneanu, Chapter 15.
Major Victor M. Rosello, "Vietnam's Support to El Salvador's FMLN," *Military Review*, January 1990, 72.

18. Tammy Arbuckle, "El Salvador, the real war in Central America?" *International Defense Review*, February 1989, 157.

19. Castellanos, 25.
Julia Preston, "Salvadoran Rebels Still Based in Nicaragua, Monitors Told," *The Washington Post*, 07 January 88, A29 & A33.

20. Castellanos, 134.
Radu and Tismaneanu, Chapter 15.

21. Castellanos, 60.
Manwaring and Prisk, 157-159.

22. Castellanos, 61.

23. Castellanos, 65.

24. "FMLN: Appeal For Sandinista Help (November 5, 1983)" and "Minutes of FMLN-Sandinista Meeting (November 7, 1983)" *The Central American Crisis Reader*, 453-458.

25. Dan Williams, "Ortega Concedes Weapons Went to Salvador Rebels," *Los Angeles* (California) *Times*, 25 June 1987, NEWSBANK 1987 INT 104:B2-3.

26. Julia Preston, "Salvadoran Rebels Still Based In Nicaragua, Monitors Told," *The Washington Post*, 07 January 1988, A29 & A33.

27. Lee Hockstadter, "Sandinistas Charged in Missiles Sale," *The Washington Post*, 03 January 1991, A15.

28. Carl von Clausewitz, *On War*, (Harmondsworth, Middlesex: Penguin Books, 1968), 119.

29. Loveman and Davies, "El Salvador" case study, *Guerrilla Warfare*, 408-409.    A dozen or so ERP members were condemned with Dalton, but only one other was actually executed. Reputedly, Villalobos shot Dalton himself.

30. Che Guevara, *Guerrilla Warfare*, with an introduction and case studies by Loveman and Davies (New York: Monthly Review Press, 1961; repr. Lincoln NE: University of Nebraska Press, 1985), 126-132.

31. Andrew Hoehn & Juan Carlos Weiss, "Overview of Latin American Insurgencies," *Latin American Insurgencies*, ed. Georges Fauriol (Washington DC: Government Printing Office, 1985), 16-17.

32. "FPL: The Revolution is the Best Medium for the Comparison of Strategic and Tactical Approaches (1978)", *The Central America Crisis Reader*, ed. Robert S. Leiken & Barry Rubin, (New York: Summit Books, 1987), 367.

33. "FPL," 367.

34. von Clausewitz, 126-127.

35. Castellanos, 62.
 Dalton appears to have been more of a revisionist *foquista* than anything else. His elevation to status of martyr within the movement appears to have been a tactical move by the FPL to support their own strategic theory and to chasten Villalobos.

36. "FPL", 368.

37. Eric Pianin, "U.S. Behind Breakins, Sanctuary Leaders Testify," *The Washington Post*, February 20, 1987, A27.
 During Congressional hearings in 1987 CISPES spokesman Michael Lent testified under oath that no link existed between CISPES and the FMLN/-FDR.

38. Van Gosse, "The North American Front: Central American Solidarity in the Reagan Era," *Reshaping the U.S. Left: Popular Struggles in the 1980s*, ed. Mike Davis & Michael Sprinkler, (New York: Verso, 1988), 35.

39. Mao Tsetung, *Quotations From Chairman Mao Tsetung*, (Peking PRC: Foreign Language Press, 1972), 58-59.
 In his essay *On Protracted War*, Mao actually quotes von Clausewitz's "politics by other means."

40. von Clausewitz, 129.
41. Castellanos, 41.

# Chapter 3

# El Salvador and the Cold War

As late as March 1977 Charles W. Bray III was able to say to a House subcommittee that the "United States has no strategic interests in El Salvador; we do have an interest in the general tranquility and progress of the region."[1] The fiscal year 1977 security assistance request was limited, and included only twelve actual weapons - jeep mounted 106mm recoilless rifles (primarily an anti-tank weapon) - the need for which was sharply questioned by the House subcommittee.[2]

The economic assistance program was described as "modest." Its focus was to "improve the quality of rural life, to support El Salvador's own family planning program, to improve the educational system and to assist in the areas of nutrition and health."[3] Permeating the discussion and conditioning everything else was the issue of human rights.

This was in accordance with Jimmy Carter's commitment, expressed during his speech at Notre Dame in May 1977, to make human rights "a cornerstone of his administration, a reaction to the brutality that afflicts the world, and to our often expedient association, in the name of national security, with rulers who do bad things to their people."[4] This commitment later led to Presidential

Decision memorandum 30 (PD-30), which set out guidelines for implementing Carter's human rights policy. That there were problems with PD-30 can be inferred by the fact that it wasn't approved until a year into the Carter Administration.

> PD-30 set out intelligent priorities, but did not resolve practical questions. The guidelines put priority on rights of the person, political liberties, and economic and social justice, in that order. The elemental issue was naked repression: torture, killing, and the disappeared, which in Latin America became a verb in the active voice, as in "The government disappeared my son," an all-too-frequent event. . . .
> PD-30 also reiterated congressional strictures against support for police functions, absent exceptional circumstances, for nations that systematically violated human rights. It did nothing, however, to settle the problem of how to define exceptional circumstances, the crux of the argument . . .[5]

In 1977 one of these practical problems reared its ugly head. It was the question of fraud and the post-election political climate in the 1977 Salvadoran elections.

> The elections have been followed by dissension among the population and repressive measures by the Government to maintain power. The unrest and disquiet of the El Salvadoran people after the elections was evidenced by a week of nonviolent demonstrations with more than 50,000 people participating on one occasion. The Government finally fired upon the demonstrators, killing at least 8 and possibly as many as 20 people and wounding some 60 persons. Approximately 200 persons were detained.[6]

The language used to describe the economic assistance thus had to be adjusted to fit the wording of the Harkin amendment to the Foreign Assistance Act, which required that "no assistance be given to a country engaged in a consistent pattern of gross violations of . . . human rights unless such aid will directly benefit the needy in that country."[7]

Key features of the policy towards El Salvador then, would seem to have been a concentration on democracy and human rights, with economic aid designed to help the rural poor, and with military aid a low priority. This was, of course, before the storm that broke over the region two years later, and especially before the 1979 coup in El Salvador itself.

**The 1979 Coup**

The proximate cause of the crisis in El Salvador was a coup on 15 October 1979 by a group of reformist Army officers. Faced with the alarming events next door in Nicaragua, they may have been attempting to preempt a similar revolution in their own country. Their reforms appear to have been mild and well-intentioned - if implemented they could have at least ameliorated the land hunger of the small farmers - but sparked uprisings by extremists of both the left and right.

> The far right was clearly opposed to their intentions because it was the Civil-Military Junta that initiated the momentous reforms in agriculture, land tenure, and banking, which were all to the elites' perceived detriment. They were opposed by the FDR and its militant arm, the FMLN, because they were co-opting the political and social rationale of the guerrilla movement and placing it within a potentially democratic context. They were opposed internally by the leadership of the armed forces, who saw a threat to their vested interests in continuing an alliance with the oligarchy that had existed for decades.[8]

The left demonstrated, the security forces reacted, and the right overreacted. What had been simmering discontent became a full boiling insurrection. "El Salvador became a polarized, fragmented society on the verge of anarchy."[9] Jose Napoleon Duarte was future president, but at that time was chiefly known as a former mayor of San Salvador and a 1972 presidential candidate who had been deprived of victory by fraud, then beaten, jailed, and exiled to Guatemala.[10] He observed that:

> The Left took strength from the chaos, from the bloodshed, the hundreds of victims each month. This made a mass insurrection more likely. The Left was counting on a broad-based uprising, not a guerrilla victory. At that time, the tiny guerrilla cells had no hope of defeating the Army. They were capable only of

destabilizing the government. Their plan was to lead a massive revolt by the population, the way the Sandinista guerrillas led the people against Somoza's dictatorship.[11]

## No More Cubas

In the political climate of the time it was impossible for the U.S. not to get involved eventually. In Nicaragua the Sandinistas were dragging their country into the Soviet bloc. What had started as a purely local revolt was redefining itself on global terms - the Sandinistas saw and presented themselves as allies of the Soviet Union and enemies of the United States. Considering the background of the FMLN and its close ties with both Cuba and the Sandinistas, it was perfectly reasonable to expect that if the FMLN ever attained power it would do the same. Thus the fact that the war in El Salvador was a civil war arising from internal problems became irrelevant. Put simply, it didn't matter who started or ran the war if the result was another pro-Soviet, anti-U.S. regime in power.

What harm could such a regime do? First, there was the credibility problem, termed "dangerous and pernicious" by Philip Berryman in his book *Inside Central America*, and attacked by him and other critics from precisely the wrong angle; that of its effect on domestic politics.[12] 'Credibility' in this sense had nothing to do with domestic politics. Allowing the FMLN to shoot its way to power would have been a serious blow to the U.S. internationally. Prestige is one of the currencies of international relations, and U.S. reserves of it were low due to the events of the disastrous 70's.[13] Considering the climate at the time of Communist expansion wherever Western response was judged to be weak, such perceptions were important.[14]

Second, there were national security concerns. These were trivialized by CISPES staff member Van Gosse with the comment that the "arms-loaded dugout canoes that cross the Gulf of Fonseca from Leninist Nicaragua to democratic El Salvador (or so the CIA maintains) might brazenly open fire on a passing US warship."[15] An only slightly less farfetched 'straw man' commonly erected by opponents to U.S. policy was the prospect of Soviet nuclear missiles being installed in El Salvador.[16] This rather bizarre scenario appears in none of the serious literature supporting U.S. policy, but is treated by critics as if it was an actual concern, and as if by debunking it they were discrediting official policy. Real strategic interests were, by ignorance or design, overlooked.

A more likely "nuclear" use of El Salvador would have been as a post-strike base for Soviet bombers in the event of nuclear war. A common argument for the categorization of the Soviet TU-22M Backfire as a tactical rather than a strategic weapon was its insufficient range to strike a target in the United States and return to a base in the Soviet Union.[17] Use of Central American airfields as post-strike bases would eliminate this problem neatly. This would also open up southern California to attack by cruise missile carrying Tu-95MS Bear-H bombers, which could fly a more survivable low-altitude ingress profile, launch from far out to sea (below the radar horizon), and have more options for egress routes, including southward.

Installation of naval facilities was another possibility. Philip Berryman made the counter-argument that "it is hard to see what that would add to what the USSR has had in Cuba for two decades."[18] This view was indeed myopic. Cuba doesn't have a Pacific coastline. El Salvador does. Availability of facilities on both the Pacific and the Caribbean would allow the Soviets more operational flexibility and broaden their scope of operations.

Dispersal of resources makes them more survivable in a wartime environment. The United States has limited resources to begin with and would be accordingly more interested in direct, current threats to the United States itself, to Japan, and to major U.S. allies in Europe. Potential threats to the south would tend to have a lower priority.

Another argument is that the revolutionary political leaders wouldn't want to make themselves and their country targets for nuclear retaliation. No evidence has ever been offered to support this view, and the only historical precedent comes from Cuba. The thought that his island might become the focus of nuclear war doesn't seem to have overly concerned Fidel Castro when Soviet missiles and bombers were being emplaced in his country; quite the opposite, he seems to have assumed that it would enhance his security.

Revolutionaries tend to be risk takers and careful weighers of odds. Soviet bases on their soil could become targets in the event of a nuclear exchange, but realistically the chances for such an exchange during the 1980s were remote, while the possibility of U.S. invasion was seen as far more likely.[19] To have a Soviet physical presence could be perceived as reducing the chances of invasion, because the United States would be risking direct confrontation with the U.S.S.R. There would also be the material benefits of generous Soviet military assistance, with Cuba and Sandinista Nicaragua serving as encouraging examples of others who had joined the 'Socialist' camp.

Similarly, the argument that the Soviets wouldn't be able to defend a far-flung outpost in someplace like Nicaragua or El Salvador misses the point. In wartime the strategic value may dissipate, but in the quasi-peace of the Cold War such a penetration into the other side's sphere of influence could be quite valuable. Soviet-bloc Cuba has been a continuous headache for U.S. policymakers. That the Soviets felt this way about penetration into their own sphere is evidenced by their behavior toward Berlin. Their first attempt to choke it off provoked the Berlin Airlift, and subsequent actions - the Berlin Wall being the best known - showed quite clearly that they took this tiny, indefensible, militarily almost helpless enclave seriously indeed.

An example closer to home is the U.S. Navy base at Guantanamo, in Cuba. The base is no direct military threat to Cuba and the Navy is there by legal agreement. But Castro has hated it since at least his guerrilla days, and the U.S. presence there has been a continuing source of friction.[20] Why? Because it is a symbol. Symbols are important in politics, and the Cold War was always fought more by chesslike political maneuver than by direct military action.

As a practical matter, Pacific ocean bases would have given the Soviet Navy - especially their AGIs (intelligence collection ships) - better access to the U.S. west coast. Similarly, a more likely prospective use of Salvadoran airfields would have been to support Soviet aerial reconnaissance efforts against the western U.S., much as Cuban bases have been used to support such activities against the eastern seaboard.[21] One of the chief U.S. objections to the expansion of Punta Huete Airfield in Nicaragua was that it could be put to just such use.[22] That it was not was probably more due to U.S. pressure than any lack of intention on the part of the Soviets.

With a second Soviet ally in Central America, certainly armed to the teeth like all Soviet satellites and swinging the regional balance of power, this pressure would be likely be seen as bearable.

Besides these possibilities, what the administration thought the Soviets were up to in a more direct and immediate fashion is set forth in a series of pamphlets, especially *The Challenge to Democracy in Central America* and *The Soviet-Cuban Connection in Central America and the Caribbean*.

> While Moscow is not likely to mount a direct military challenge to the United States in the Caribbean Basin, it is attempting to foment as much unrest as possible in an area that is the strategic crossroads of the Western Hemisphere: the narrow straits of Florida, which pass by Cuba, would be the principle route to Europe of U.S. troop and supply ships carrying 60% of the reinforcements and supplies to NATO during a European emergency. Moreover, almost half of U.S. imports and exports are transported through these waters, and two out of every three ships transiting the Panama Canal carry goods to or from the United States. More than half of the imported petroleum required by the United States passes through these waters. Working through Cuba, the Soviet Union hopes to force the United States to divert attention to an area that in the past has not been a serious security concern.[23]

Arkady Shevchenko's revelations about Soviet activities and the Soviet interpretation of detente would tend to support such a view of their meddling in Central America. There was also a commitment in Soviet military doctrine to support 'wars of national liberation.' To cap this the Soviet Minister of Defense, Marshal A. A. Grechko, made some uncomfortable statements about Soviet power projection capabilities in 1974 in the Soviet journal *Problems of History of the CPSU*.

> At the present stage the historic function of the Soviet Armed Forces is not restricted to their function of defending our Motherland and the other socialist countries. In its foreign policy activity the Soviet state purposefully opposes the export of counterrevolution and the policy of oppression, supports the national liberation struggle, and resolutely resists imperialists' aggression in whatever distant region of our planet it may appear.[24]

Which leads to the regional threat. This was the problem of likely Salvadoran support for Marxist insurgencies in neighboring countries, in much the same way as the Cubans and Sandinistas did in Honduras and El Salvador itself.[25] Berryman pooh-poohed this notion on the grounds that revolution is not caused by the revolutionaries themselves, but by objective conditions of social change, and that the revolutionaries are not "part of a monolithic global communist movement" with a timetable for world conquest.[26] These are not sound arguments.

Cuban 'Foco' theory, which long dominated the thinking of Latin American revolutionaries (and which is still influential), holds that revolution *is* sparked by small bands of dedicated revolutionaries. Che Guevara wrote that "[i]t is not necessary to wait until all conditions for making revolution exist; the insurrection can create them."[27] There is also a presupposition in Berryman's argument that any nation suffering from an insurgency must be so socially unjust as to deserve it. This smacks of blaming the victim, and does not explain, for example, the Uruguayan National Liberation Movement - Tupamaros (MLN), which arose in what was probably the most open, socially equitable society in South America (albeit one undergoing economic turmoil at the time).[28]

As for the 'monolithic global communist movement,' no one has seriously suggested such a thing since the early 1960s. What has been proven to exist was a series of interlocking networks, which connected Marxist revolutionary movements and was supported by the USSR, Cuba, and the rest of the Soviet bloc.[29] Finally, the FMLN itself clearly stated a commitment to spread its revolution beyond the borders of El Salvador.

> This is not just a Salvadoran revolution. We have to help all of the oppressed and exploited people of Latin America. After we triumph here we will go to Guatemala and offer our proletarian brothers the benefit of our experience. . . . Eventually we will fight in Mexico.[30]

There was also a prospective conventional threat, highlighted by the Sandinistas receiving a huge tank force from the Soviet Union as one of the first items of military aid. Large armored forces are of peripheral value in a counterinsurgency, but are excellent as weapons of intimidation and invasion, and the Soviets had a history of providing them to new allies. Assuming that a Marxist El Salvador received the same amount of aid as Nicaragua, their combined armies, in brotherly solidarity, would have had an armored assault force with three and a half times as many tanks alone as the rest of Central America put together.[31] Such a regional threat would directly engage United States treaty obligations with the other nations of the region, much as it did in El Salvador.

**Treaty Obligations**

The legal basis for U.S. involvement is found in the Inter-American Treaty of Reciprocal Assistance (the Rio Treaty). The problem with the Rio Treaty from the U.S. point of view is that it largely overlooks internal strife, the main thrust being collective security against external aggression.[32] The Central American Defense Council (CONDECA) was organized by El Salvador, Guatemala, Honduras, and Nicaragua on 2 July 1963, specifically against "possible communist aggression." The United States is not a formal member, but strongly influenced its formation. CONDECA fell into decline in the late 1960's, but "was revived on Oct. 2, 1983, by El Salvador, Guatemala, and Honduras in order to achieve a joint approach to any 'extra-continental aggression of a Marxist-Leninist character'."[33]

This may be why external support for the FMLN was so strongly emphasized by the U.S., and presented as a direct attack on El Salvador. Under the provisions of the Rio Treaty, the validity of the legal basis is made stronger by an interpretation of the FMLN's activities as an act of external aggression; a debatable point. However, if U.S. support for the Nicaraguan 'Contra' rebels could be considered aggression against Sandinista Nicaragua, then similarly, Soviet bloc, Cuban and Sandinista support for the FMLN could be seen as aggression against El Salvador. This may be why the Sandinistas and their U.S. allies insisted, in the face of all evidence, that "the Sandinistas do not supply arms to the FMLN: never have, never will."[34]

Thus U.S. intervention in the Salvadoran civil war was not only legal, but obligatory under standing treaties. Actually, though, none of this legalistic maneuvering particularly mattered so long as the strategic basis for involvement was still valid. Basically it was a 'fig leaf' to cover an operation based on strategic concerns.

**Reagan Policy**

The resultant 'Reagan Policy' was actually a natural outgrowth of the 'Carter Policy,' mutated by the tumultuous events of the late 1970's. The human rights policy came under particular attack during the presidential campaign, but, as Frank McNeil observes, "in office the Reagan administration kept a semblance of the policy."[35] Another influence was the President's National Bipartisan Commission on Central America, chaired by Henry Kissinger, which reported its findings in 1984.[36]

Jack Child, in his 1985 article "US Policies Toward Insurgencies in Latin America," called the then-current U.S. Central American policy "a reasonable and balanced mix of the '4 d's'," Democracy, Development, Diplomacy, and Defense. He described this policy as a "middle course," one of several possible options between withdrawal and military intervention. He was concerned about "The degree to which this stated policy is actually being carried out, the priority of military solutions subsumed under 'defense,' and the extent to which a multilateral negotiation solution has sincerely been sought . . ."[37]

Mr. Child felt that the Kissinger Commission's recommendations were another balanced approach, differing only in emphasis from the pre-existing official policy. "[I]t essentially advocates reform in the Alliance for Progress tradition, using development and democracy as counterinsurgency instruments, with emphasis on the military element."[38] The concrete form of this "instrument" was the Caribbean Basin Initiative, which was seen by many observers as virtually the Alliance For Progress reborn.[39] An apparent synthesis of the official policy and the Kissinger Commission's recommendations was summarized in *The Challenge to Democracy in Central America*, published in June 1986.

> **Democracy** is central to this policy, for the United States believes that governments that evolve from the ballot box are not

only respectful of the rights of their citizens, but also of the rights of neighboring countries. . . Democracy, however, is not an end; it is a fragile process that requires careful nurturing and constant attention. Democracy seeks to give political power to the people and their representatives, not solely to the elites of the political extremes.

**Economic** development is essential, for poverty and social injustice provide communism the opportunity to provoke violence and subversion. U.S. development policy is aimed at bettering the life of the people of the region and replacing frustration with hope. . . . The goal of the United States is to help these countries achieve self-sustaining economic growth to enable them to provide jobs and opportunity to their citizens.

**Diplomacy** recognizes that dialogue can be a prelude to peace, and that words are preferable to bullets. But the words must be followed by actions and tied to a genuine, lasting peace, not a transient truce that masks continued aggression. A regional peaceful solution can best be attained through the Contadora process, and internally by a dialogue between the governments and the insurgent movements in their countries. Meaningful dialogue could lead insurgent groups to lay down their weapons and compete safely and fairly within a democratically based political process.

**Defense** is necessary to provide the countries of the region with the arms and military training to defend themselves. U.S. military assistance is a shield behind which the other elements of the policy are protected. U.S. economic aid alone to these countries will have little impact against guerrillas provided with large quantities of arms and ammunition by Cuba, Nicaragua, and the rest of the Communist bloc.[40]

The '4 d's' were still present, but Jack Child's concerns about the priority and precise meaning of 'defense' were well founded. This problem was exacerbated by a weakness he identified in the original plan, which was also carried over into the 1986 policy. Child was concerned that there appeared to be no backup plan in case "the chosen US regional allies turn out to be supporters of the status quo instead of reformers."[41] According to Benjamin C. Schwartz in the Rand study *American Counterinsurgency Doctrine and El Salvador*, the Salvadoran political right was perfectly willing to accept U.S. material aid, but much less enthusiastic about U.S. advice on reforming their country.

> . . . [T]he democratic process itself has served to thwart American plans and hopes for reform in El Salvador. . . . The rightists' obstructionist parliamentary tactics . . . severely curtailed the Christian Democrats' ability to enact reforms, and the right cooperated with the government only to the extent its members believed essential to maintain American economic and military assistance. Moreover, despite the centrists' majority in the legislature, the rightists retained control of the courts, resulting in the frustrating failures to punish human rights violators . . .[42]

U.S. policy was stymied by Central American politics, much as it had been in Nicaragua a half-century earlier. Not only did the U.S. find itself being dragged along by a "weaker ally," but one containing elements only slightly less inimical than the FMLN.[43] The solutions to El Salvador's problems seemed so obvious that the lack of cooperation was maddening. Certainly, there would be some inconvenience, but didn't these people realize that it was for their own good?

As Schwartz points out, it is very difficult to get a sovereign, foreign nation to do what you want it to. Contrary to FMLN propaganda, the Salvadoran government was assuredly not a puppet of the United States.[44] And in El Salvador powerful segments of the politically active population had solid reasons for not going along with U.S. advice. Essentially, to do so would entail losing a favorable status quo: the very thing they were fighting the FMLN to keep.[45]

Related to this was the fact that the U.S. and El Salvador were fighting two different wars, which did not completely match up on all points. For the U.S. it was a small campaign in a global war with the Soviet Union, while for El Salvador it was a local war for political control. Put another way, the United States opposed the FMLN because it was an ally of the Soviet Union, while the Salvadoran government opposed the Soviet Union because it was an ally of the FMLN.

Because of this perceptual difference, the allies' interpretations of the relative importance of defense were poles apart. For the U.S. policymakers, defense was a short-term item; as it says, a "shield" behind which the long-term solutions could be carried out. The Salvadoran right saw reform as only slightly less threatening than revolution, and favored military defeat of the rebels. And by the very nature of the U.S. interpretation of the conflict, the right could not be effectively compelled to comply with the U.S. program.

> Committing American prestige and influence by vowing to "draw a line" against communism is not the best way to ensure leverage over an ally. As Salvadoran officials assert, throughout the 1980s they did not "take the [American] threats to punish the military by cutting off aid seriously because they believed the U.S. stake in stopping Marxist expansionism was so great that help would continue."[46]

Included in Jack Child's critique of U.S. policy was a suggestion that an alternative would be to "de-emphasize the 'defense' portion and replace it with 'de-militarization'."[47] This might, in fact, have sidestepped the trap Morgenthau warned against, where the U.S. could neither "retreat without losing face" nor "advance without grave risks."[48]

> An alternative middle course would stress ways of defusing tensions instead of igniting them. All parties would seek to return Central American problems to their lower historical level by decoupling them from outside issues and forces; means would be sought to verify negotiable solutions while protecting legitimate interests.[49]

Clearly, then, "outside issues and forces" were seen as significant stumbling blocks to peace in Central America, because the East-West conflict had taken priority over the North-South orientation that the Carter administration had been cautiously developing.[50] 'Decoupling' the local conflict from them would allow more room for maneuver, but how to go about doing that was as much a problem as the one which led to it. At least it was until 1989.

In the late 1980s the Communist bloc began to crack, crumble, and collapse. Except in such politically backwards enclaves as North Korea, Vietnam, China, Cuba and Berkeley, it became clear that Communism had discredited itself, and the Cold War was essentially over. As an unintended result, the East-West issues that had bogged down U.S. Central American policy decoupled themselves from the Salvadoran civil war. The balance of power had clearly swung to the United States, and national interest was no longer served by fighting Communist guerrillas in El Salvador.

## Notes

1. United States Congress House Subcommittee on Inter-American Affairs, *The Recent Presidential Elections in El Salvador, Implications for U.S. Foreign Policy*, (Washington DC: Government Printing Office, 1977), 4.

2. House Subcommittee on Inter-American Affairs, 4.

3. House Subcommittee on Inter-American Affairs, 4.

4. McNeil, 92.

5. McNeil, 94.

6. House Subcommittee on Inter-American Affairs, 2.

7. House Subcommittee on Interamerican Affairs, 6.

8. Dr. Alvaro Magana, "By 1979, the Situation Was Beyond Control by Repression," *El Salvador at War*, ed. Max G. Manwaring and Court Prisk, with a preface by Edwin G. Corr (Washington DC: National Defense University Press, 1988), 29-30.

9. Max G. Manwaring and Court Prisk, *El Salvador at War*, with a preface by Ambassador Edwin G. Corr (Washington, D.C.: National Defense University Press, 1988), 36.

10. General Fred F. Woerner, "The Leadership Was in Limbo", *El Salvador at War*, 34.

11. President Jose Napoleon Duarte, *Duarte: My Story* (New York: G.P. Putnam's Sons, 1986), 106-107.

12. Berryman, 99.

13. Joseph Cirincione and Leslie C. Hunter, "Military Threats, Actual and Potential," *Central America - Anatomy of a Conflict*, ed. Robert S. Leiken (Elmsford NY: Pergamon Press, 1984), 174.

14. Rick Marshall, "Is Co-existence Possible in Central America?" *Defense & Foreign Affairs*, December 1984, 12.

15. Van Gosse, 12.

16. Berryman, 98.

17. Steven Zaloga, "The Tu-22M 'Backfire' Bomber - Part 2," *Jane's Intelligence Review*, August 1992, 345.

18. Berryman, 86.

19. Van Gosse, 32.
After the Grenada invasion the Sandinistas whipped up a great deal of panic over a supposedly imminent U.S. invasion of Nicaragua. This propaganda - the same sort that Castro has used for thirty years, despite asserting from the other side of his mouth that he had U.S. guarantees after the missile crisis that it would never happen - was promulgated as fact by such groups as the Pledge of Resistance. Actually, there is no evidence this was contemplated.

20. Szulc, 733.

21. Joseph Cirincione and Leslie C. Hunter, "Military Threats, Actual and Potential," *Central America - Anatomy of a Conflict*, ed. Robert S. Leiken (Elmsford NY: Pergamon Press, 1984), 182.

22. Department of State and Department of Defense, *The Challenge to Democracy in Central America*, (Washington, D.C.: Government Printing Office, 1986), 27.

23. *The Challenge to Democracy in Central America*, 3-4.

24. Harriet Fast Scott & William F. Scott, *The Armed Forces of the USSR*, (Boulder CO: Westview Press, 1984), 59.

25. Rick Marshall, "Is Co-existence Possible in Central America?" *Defense & Foreign Affairs*, December 1984, 14.

26. Berryman, 95-97.

27. Guevara, 47.

28. Michael Radu & Vladimir Tismaneanu, *Latin American Revolutionaries: Groups, Goals, Methods*, (Washington DC: Pergamon-Brassey's, 1990), 347-353.

29. Ra'anan, Pfaltzgraff, et al, 8-12.

30. FMLN Commandante Neto, *San Diego Union*, March 1, 1981, 1.
As quoted by J. Michael Waller, *The Third Current of Revolution*, (Lanham MD: University Press of America, 1991), 226.

31. *The Challenge to Democracy in Central America*, 20.
Nicaragua received 350 tanks, mostly T-55's but some light reconnaissance PT-76's as well. The rest of Central America had, at that time, 200 tanks, all of them lighter in armor and armament than the T-55.

32. Henry W. Degenhardt, *Treaties and Alliances of the World - 4th Edition*, ed. Alan J. Day (Detroit: Gale Research Company, 1986), 342-343.

33. Degenhardt, 365.

34. Chuck Kaufman, spokesman for the Nicaragua Network, telephone interview by writer, 17 April 1991.
The term "Nicaragua Network" is a misnomer. The organization actually supports the Sandinistas. It also performs "coalition activity" with CISPES, although it officially "has no position on the FMLN"- (!).

35. Frank McNeil, *War and Peace in Central America* (New York: Charles Scribner's Sons, 1988), 93.

36. Department of State and Department of Defense, *The Challenge to Democracy in Central America*, (Washington, D.C.: Government Printing Office, 1986), 1-2.

37. Jack Child, "US Policies Toward Insurgencies in Latin America," *Latin American Insurgencies*, Georges Fauriol, ed., (Washington DC: Government Printing Office, 1985), 154.

38. Child, 155.

39. Ronald Reagan, "Caribbean Basin Initiative," *The Central America Crisis Reader*, ed. Robert S. Leiken & Barry Rubin, (New York: Summit Books, 1987), 528-531.
This was unveiled by President Reagan during a speech to the Organization of American States, February 24, 1982.

40. *The Challenge to Democracy in Central America*, 1-2.

41. Child, 155.

42. Benjamin C. Schwartz, *American Counterinsurgency Doctrine and El Salvador*, (Santa Monica CA: RAND, 1991), 59.

43. This refers to Morganthau's rule of never letting a weaker ally make decisions for you.
Rightist elements murdered seven Americans, and are suspect in two more cases; the last of them in 1982.

44. Castellanos, 23.

45. Schwartz, 61-62.

46. Schwartz, 61-62.

47. Child, 154.

48. Morganthau, 589.

49. Child, 155.

50. Considering Jimmy Carter's track record on just two emotive issues - the Panama Canal and Cuba - it is interesting to speculate how far he might have gotten had detente been what the West thought it was.

# Chapter 4

# Private Foreign Policy

The basis of U.S. policy towards El Salvador was, quite properly, national security. The significant domestic opposition (of varying degrees of loyalty) to that policy had its own agenda ostensibly based on idealism, predominately the issues of 'human rights' and 'non-intervention.'[1] Determining the precise content of this counterpolicy is somewhat difficult in that there is, obviously, no single authority to refer to. Most opponents of U.S. policy however, seem to have been broadly in agreement with the 'revolutionary policy' discussed below. Their own contribution seems to have been more a common set of general attitudes, expressed as a series of slogans and key words, rather than a thoughtful program. The simplest expressions of the two concerns mentioned above were, respectively, "no aid to the death-squad government of El Salvador," and "no more Vietnams."

**Revolutionary Policy**

Obviously, the most direct counterpolicy would be that of the revolutionaries themselves. Phillip Berryman, in his 1985 book *Inside Central America*, attempted to formulate this policy "on the basis of Sandinista government programs, documents of the Salvadoran and Guatemalan revolutionary movements, and analyses by Central American social scientists."

### An End to Violence

Out of a concern to address the political and economic issues, the number one aspiration of people in Central America might be overlooked: peace. The basic reason for violence in Central America today is resistance to change on the part of those holding economic power. . . .

### A New Economic Model

All observers recognize that any solution in Central America must entail economic change. . . Central American revolutionaries hope to foment a new kind of mixed economy with strong state participation that will reorient production toward meeting basic needs . . . and at the same time lay the groundwork for further integrated development.

### Political Participation

Strictly speaking, the political system of sovereign countries are internal matters - except where gross violations of human rights become a matter of concern of the international community. Thus, in principle, which political forms a revolutionary government adopts should not be of direct concern to U.S. policy. . .  .[2]

### Nonalignment

The Sandinistas and the revolutionary opposition movements in El Salvador and Guatemala see themselves as part of the Third World and would describe their approach to foreign policy as "nonalignment." . . . the United States would have to acknowledge the right to genuine nonalignment, including the right to maintain trade and diplomatic relations with socialist countries.[3]

Berryman did qualify this plan with a parenthetical comment that "whether they will work is a separate question."[4] This is fortunate for him, because there are serious problems and objections to the "revolutionary" policy. Taking them briefly, point by point, these are some:

Peace: The violence was by no means confined to the 'traditional' regimes. The FMLN systematically engaged in political murder. The Sandinistas also have a history of political assassinations, including the gruesome torture-murder of 'Commandante Bravo,' Pablo Emilio Salazar, on October 10, 1979 in Tegucigalpa, Honduras. According to Arturo Cruz, then a Sandinista, "the Sandinistas captured and tortured Bravo, slowly protracting his death. In the process, Bravo's face was ripped off. The intention was not only to kill him but to send a clear message to anyone so disposed to challenge the regime." . . .[5]

Economy: As a revolutionary movement in power during this period the Sandinistas must serve as the working model of this ideal Central American economy. Put simply, it did not work.[6]

Political Participation: The FMLN has a history of hostility towards elections in its country, and the writings of Joaquin Villalobos would indicate that they would prefer something closer to the Cuban model.[7] That this form of government would bear little or no relationship to representative democracy is implied by Berryman's statement above (which seems designed to forestall criticism), and confirmed by Castro's comment that "Western democracy has nothing to do with real democracy. It's complete garbage."[8]

Nonalignment: One of the greatest farces of international relations was Cuba's status of 'nonalignment.' Cuba was, of course, as close an ally of the Soviet Union as any member of the Warsaw Pact (possibly closer than Romania). It would be natural to expect a new revolutionary regime with close ties to Cuba to be just as 'nonaligned.'

**Principled Realism**

There were several attempts to develop coherent, reasonable alternatives to the current policy. One of the better ones, termed 'principled realism,' is outlined in *Confronting Revolution*, published in 1986.

> 1. The foremost long-term objective of U.S. policy must be to promote broadly shared development and encourage democracy. While not ignoring the East-West dimension of regional conflict, such a policy would recognize that this aspect is secondary. . . .

> 2. Diplomatic solutions should be a primary objective of U.S. policy. . . . The escalation and internationalization of regional conflict presents the greatest danger of superpower involvement and confrontation.
>
> 3. We should refrain from undertaking any policy that is unable to garner allied support, except in the most extraordinary circumstances where there is a direct and immediate danger to U.S. security. . . .
>
> 4. The United States should work diplomatically, in concert with our allies, to change the behavior of any regime which is a gross and systematic violator of human rights or which enforces deep social inequality by repressive means. . . .
>
> 5. The United States should apply the same policy principles to all countries. . . .The interests of the United States are not automatically endangered by revolutionary regimes.[9]

Although borrowing the term 'realism' as it relates to foreign policy, use of the term 'principled' implies adherence to an ideal.[10] Examination of the basic tenets above suggests that the principle involved is leftist. The 'revolutionary policy's' combination of hostility toward 'traditional' regimes and sympathy for 'revolutionary' regimes and groups is more muted, but clearly present.

There is a certain amount of agreement between this and official policy. Specifically addressing the problem of El Salvador, the authors of 'principled realism' proposed that they would "seek a negotiated settlement of the Salvadoran conflict, rather than seeking military victory for the existing regime."[11] This is in line with Child's suggestion of 'de-militarization,' and quite close to a State Department policy statement by U.S. Ambassador to the Organization of American States Luigi Einaudi some five years later. The Ambassador called for "A negotiated political solution and a cease-fire leading to free elections" during an address before the Permanent Council of the OAS on February 14, 1991.[12]

It is significant that this came about after the radical political changes of 1989-1990. On a global level, the Soviet Union had removed itself as a threat and its principal ally in the region, the Sandinistas, had been voted out of office in Nicaragua. On the local level, the Soviets had quit supplying the FMLN, and the Sandinistas' supply effort was crippled.

This view on a negotiated peace seems finally to have been accepted by the Salvadoran government, including - most importantly - the Army. In an interview with *Jane's Defence Weekly* just before the November 1989 FMLN 'Final Offensive,' Army Chief of Staff Colonel Rene Emilio Ponce stated that "we have come to realise that this war is to a great extent political in nature, and we would be foolish to simply seek a military solution."[13]

One problem with the concept of negotiations is that, much as the U.S. and U.S.S.R. saw detente differently, the rebels and the Salvadoran Government saw 'negotiations' differently. Using the training they had received from Vietnam, the FMLN used negotiations as a tactic. These 'negotiations' gave them excellent propaganda, a breathing space to organize for their next offensive, and a chance to bully concessions from the government. Observers noted just before the 1989 'Final Offensive' that FMLN negotiators suddenly became more rigid and demanding, as if they were trying to force the government to break off the talks.[14] Apparently they were, as an excuse to launch their long planned offensive and with the hope of having a propaganda advantage when they did. Although 'negotiations' was an important issue for the U.S. support networks, how both they and the FMLN actually felt about them was revealed by FMLN Diplomatic/Political Commission member Salvador Samayoa during a meeting with U.S. activists on September 22, 1990.

> We devised a scheme of failure and deadlock, and we were able to avoid the deadline that we had for the middle of September. Now we are going to be able to play it more at ease during the negotiation. This is going to have a longer term. We won't have meetings every three weeks, which was a drag, and the next meeting is programmed for November. So now this process is going to continue in a slower pace and in harmony with the revolutionary strategy of the FMLN.[15]

If such a reasoned approach as "principled realism" had dominated the dialogue between proponents and opponents of official policy, a synthesis of thought and consensus on aims might have resulted. Instead the matter became a cause celebre of the radical left, and, as in the case of Vietnam, the role of the principal opponents to U.S. policy shifted from a position of loyal dissent to that of advocacy for the other side.

## An Attitude as Much as a Policy

The views of this movement can be condensed to a few sentences. What follows is necessarily general, but exceptions are rare, due to the surprising ideological homogeneity of the movement.

1. Revolution was preferable to reform.

2. The movement had an active, simplistic hostility towards the elected government of El Salvador and its armed forces, and was deeply suspicious of - and often equally hostile toward - the institutions of its own country, especially the U.S. military.

3. It supported the Sandinistas, often using the term 'the elected government of Nicaragua', and condemned their opposition (the 'Contra') as terrorist. This support was also evident for other 'progressive' governments, particularly Castro's Cuba but also other Soviet bloc and client states.

4. Capitalism was seen as evil, tied inevitably to 'imperialism.'

5. The terms 'peace,' 'democracy,' 'human rights,' 'non-intervention' and 'the People' were used a great deal, although interpretation of these terms (especially 'democracy') was often rather exotic.

6. Even the supposedly Christian groups such as Pax Christi and Quixote Center espoused the view that anyone who didn't support the extreme (and violent) left was automatically a supporter of the extreme right, justifying their support for the FMLN/FDR with the comment that "the other side killed more."[16]

7. In public statements network organizations rarely told the whole truth about their and the FMLN/FDR's aims, political nature, and relationship.

To reference the movement's 'counter-policy' specifically to the statement of official policy and to El Salvador, it aimed to strip away the 'shield' and apply pressure to the Salvadoran government until the latter, essentially, surrendered. That this policy, if successful, could have lead to an FMLN victory was of varying concern to the groups involved. Some were openly hoping for a revolution along Cuban and Sandinista lines, while others were ostensibly more moderate.

## Notes

1. Van Gosse, 12.

Van Gosse asserted that there was a "sterile division" between "solidarity" and "non-intervention" branches of the movement, but in practice these groups merged and their propaganda approach was based predominately on the two issues of "human rights" and "non-intervention."

2. There is a certain amount of hypocrisy inherent in this statement. If the forms a revolutionary government takes are not to be the business of outsiders, then why are the forms of government taken by "traditional" regimes such a matter of concern? Berryman is saying that intervention is objectively wrong, except under the conditions dictated here. This "something is an objective evil except when our side does it" mentality is common throughout the counterpolicy groups.

3. Phillip Berryman, *Inside Central America* (New York: Pantheon Books, 1985), 100-106.

4. Berryman, 100.

5. Arturo Cruz, Jr., *Memoirs of a Counterrevolutionary* (New York: Doubleday, 1989), 122.

6. David Brock, "The Poverty of a Failed Revolution," *Insight*, 31 October 1988, 36-38.

7. Joaquin Villalobos, "A Democratic Revolution For El Salvador," *Foreign Policy* 74 (Spring 1989): 109.

8. Andres Oppenheimer, *Castro's Final Hour* (New York: Simon & Schuster, 1992), caption photo 32.

9. Morris J. Blachman, William M. Leogrande and Kenneth E. Sharpe, eds. *Confronting Revolution: Security Through Diplomacy in Central America* (New York: Pantheon Books, 1986), 351-352.

10. The general term "principled realism" could be also used to describe, more honestly, both the Reagan and Carter policies. Both adhered to certain "principles."

11. Blachman, Leogrande & Sharpe, 362.

12. Luigi R. Einaudi, "Peace and the Consolidation of Democracy in El Salvador," repr. *Dispatch* Vol. 2, No. 8 (February 25, 1991).

13. Joel Millman, "No Military Solution for El Salvador," *Jane's Defence Weekly*, 02 December 1989, 1226.

14. Millman, 1226.

15. J. Michael Waller, *The Third Current of Revolution*, (Lanham MD: University Press of America, 1991), 229.

16. This is a direct quote from a telephone interview with a spokesperson from Pax Christi, 9 February 1993.
The sentiment is a common one among the FMLN support groups, and appears to be based on the rather grisly assumption that the side with the lower body count must be the most moral. In the case of U.S. citizens, it is also incorrect. The FMLN killed at least 14 Americans, while the death squads are believed to have murdered 7 (the last in 1981), and the Salvadoran Army killed 2, only one of which was under suspicious circumstances. The big difference is that there were investigations and trials of the death squad and Army killings, while the FMLN boasted of murdering Americans and promised to murder more.

**Chapter 5**

# Organizations Opposing U.S. Policy

· This movement manifested itself as a plethora of organizations in the U.S., most of them leftist, and some of which unabashedly supported the FMLN. Van Gosse divided the movement into 'solidarity' and 'anti-intervention' forces, but didn't see that there was any practical difference between the two.

> On the one hand were those who supported the revolutionary projects, including the armed struggle, as defined by the vanguard political-military fronts in each country; on the other were those who 'only' wanted their government to adopt an enlightened policy of non-intervention and respect for self-determination. In fact, the difference was mutual stylistic discomfort. Solidarity activists were committed to a posture of enthusiastic and continual militance [sic] on behalf of the anti-imperial revolution. Anti-intervention workers often came from the older, more experienced peace movement which favored persuasion over confrontation, and a carefully 'American,' humanitarian approach. Now most people at both national and local levels have come to recognize, as the Right has charged all along, that the results for Central America are likely to be the same: hindering intervention means 'one, two, many' popular victories in the long run.[1]

Together they formed the 'army' of the U.S. front in the Salvadoran civil war, and their members were its footsoldiers, as much a part of the FMLN's war effort as the 'commandos' who machine-gunned restaurants and buses in San Salvador. Central to this complex was the 'Committee In Solidarity with the People of El Salvador,' CISPES.

## Committee in Solidarity with the People of El Salvador

Much as the Holy Roman Empire was not holy, Roman, nor an empire, CISPES was actually in solidarity with the FMLN/FDR, which it considered to be the true representative of 'the People of El Salvador.'[2] According to information from Farid Handal's captured trip report, CISPES was "formed in 1980 as the result of meetings between a representative of the FMLN/FDR and officials of the Cuban United Nations Mission, the Communist Party USA [CPUSA] and the United States Peace Council [USPC], a branch of the Moscow - controlled World Peace Council."[3] Some doubt has been cast on these connections, especially by CISPES and its supporters attempting to discredit the document itself. Most of the information has, however, been confirmed through other sources.[4] CISPES itself claimed to have been "established as a result of the U.S. National Conference in Solidarity with the Salvadoran People . . . to provide international support to the anti-government movement in El Salvador."[5] This was true as far as it went, but left out was that three of its organizers were Isabel Letelier of the Institute of Policy Studies (IPS), Robert Armstrong of the North American Council on Latin America (NACLA), and Sandy Pollack of the Communist Party USA (CPUSA) and one of its fronts, the US Peace Council (USPC).[6]

The Institute of Policy Studies is a radical left think-tank "in Washington but not of it."[7] Actually, it is very much 'of' the liberal elite of Washington, and has close ties with many in Congress. It also has (or has had) close ties with the KGB, the Cuban DGI, the PLO, Qaddafi, and a wide assortment both domestic and foreign radical Marxist groups, including the FMLN.[8] NACLA was formed virtually as a New Left intelligence agency, but soon advanced to more direct action, according to one of its own spokesmen.[9]

> The North American Congress on Latin America seeks the participation and support of men and women, from a variety of organizations and movements, who not only favor revolutionary change in Latin America but also take a revolutionary position toward their own society. . . .
> In the context of this involvement in the revolutionary struggle at home, NACLA is exploring possibilities for maintaining relationships with Latin American organizations. . . .[10]

In 1991 CISPES claimed 60,000 members, of whom 20,000 were characterized as 'active.'[11] If true, this could mean that by then there were more hard-core supporters of the FMLN in the U.S. than in El Salvador (*see Chapter 8*). It had "56 chapters and 450 affiliate groups that are ready to organize grassroots protest in hundreds of cities nationwide."[12] Many of these affiliates were also spinoffs of the IPS, such as Policy Alternatives for the Caribbean and Central America (PACCA), which was, incidentally, also affiliated with the Sandinista Regional Coordination for Economic and Social Research (CRIES).[13] Another was Neighbor to Neighbor (N2N - their abbreviation), which was organized by the Institute for Food and Development Policy (IFDP), itself an IPS spinoff (and also associated with CRIES).[14]

CISPES and its affiliates were allowed to pretend that no direct link existed between them and the FMLN/FDR. This was apparently based on CISPES not being in the direct chain of command; they 'cooperated' and 'supported' rather than taking direct orders, which theoretically allowed them to be considered independent. In a practical sense this is absurd, legalistic way of looking at it. Within the FMLN itself the different factions coordinated activities rather than operating under a strict, linear chain of command; their relationship was more parallel than hierarchal.[15] The association between the military (FMLN) and political (FDR) branches of the organization was loose and even prickly at times.[16] Thus the relationship between CISPES and the FMLN/FDR as a whole was probably as close as the relationship between the FMLN and the FDR separately.

## Movement Characteristics

A 'Vietnam Connection' appears here as well as in the FMLN. Many of the same people and organizations who were active in the Vietnam protest movement later adopted the cause of the FMLN. Ron Dellums, Democratic Congressman from Berkeley, worked extensively with CISPES and related organizations in fundraising and propaganda. During the Vietnam war he attended the Communist-organized Stockholm Conference on Vietnam as a delegate, on the strength of his association with west coast 'New Mobe' (New Mobilization Committee to End the War in Vietnam) activities.[17] The New Mobe itself was associated with the Black Panther Party, the Communist Party USA (CPUSA), the Progressive Labor Party, the Socialist Workers Party, and the Students for a Democratic Society (SDS), among less well known organizations.[18] The Communist Party USA and Students for a Democratic Society were known terrorist organizations at the time, and the CPUSA was also known as one of the most rigidly Moscow-line Communist Parties in the world.[19]

Some of the U.S. groups associated with CISPES and the FMLN were also considered to be terrorist. One of the things which spurred on the FBI investigation of CISPES was a series of bombings in and around Washington, DC, in late 1983. These were committed by the 'Armed Resistance Unit' which claimed to be doing so in solidarity with the Salvadoran people.[20] The ARU (also known as the May 19 Communist Organization) was the east coast branch of the Prairie Fire Organizing Committee, an organization with direct contacts with the FMLN and connections with both CISPES and the supposedly nonviolent Pledge of Resistance.[21]

> On the east coast is the May 19 Communist Organization. M19CO is also known as the Armed Resistance, United Revolutionary Fighting Group, and the Red Guerrilla Resistance. The M19CO is a Marxist-Leninist organization with ties to the FALN [Puerto Rican 'Armed Forces of National Liberation']. Their few members were members of the Weather Underground Organization and the Black Liberation Army. The M19CO counterpart on the west coast is the Prairie Fire Organizing Committee.[22]

According to Peter Collier and David Horowitz, the Prairie Fire Organizing Committee "was created as a traditional Communist-front organization . . ."[23] It was an outgrowth of the distribution network for a book by the 'Weathermen' (Weather Underground Organization - WUO), apparently intended to be the 'little red book' of the American Left, called *Prairie Fire*.

> Bound in red covers, *Prairie Fire* was a series of short courses on revolution, racism, imperialism, and Vietnam, along with a lengthy history of the American Left written in such a way as to suggest that they [the Weathermen] were the logical heirs of all its traditions. The dedication page listed, along with others, John Brown and Sirhan, the San Quentin Six, and the Symbionese Liberation Army. The message was summed up in the question-begging catchphrase: "Without mass struggle there can be no revolution. Without armed struggle there can be no victory."[24]

Turning to individuals, Carroll Ishee had a particularly checkered career, being involved in Vietnam protest and 'national liberation' movements in Africa, and finally being killed in combat in El Salvador while with the FMLN.[25] Daniel Ellsberg is well known for his theft of the classified 'Pentagon Papers', an action he intended to undercut the U.S. Vietnam War effort,[26] and claimed to have "been involved with the Pledge [of Resistance] from the beginning . . ."[27] Dr. Charles Clements, a conscientious objector during the Vietnam War, worked directly with the FMLN in El Salvador, wrote a book about his experiences (*Witness to War*), and later became involved with the FMLN support group Medical Aid for El Salvador (MAES).[28]

There was a great deal of overlap between organizations, which, among other things, makes an evaluation of their membership and support difficult. Ed Asner did a great deal of work for CISPES, but also worked for Medical Aid For El Salvador (MAES), Nicaragua Medical Aid (NMA) and was on the Nicaragua Network's advisory board.[29] Patricia Schroeder (D-CO), participated in fundraising for the Nicaragua Network, CISPES, and Medical Aid for El Salvador, which is only to be expected because of her long, close relationship with the Institute for Policy Studies, which organization almost seems to serve as a springboard into the world of the radical left.[30] At times organizations shared facilities as well as membership, as evidenced by CISPES (in Berkeley) and the East Bay Action Coalition on Central America having the same address and telephone number.

**Case Study: Omaha Central America Response Team**

In Omaha, Nebraska, the local official affiliate of CISPES was called Nebraskans For Peace, while the local branch of the Nicaragua Network was the Omaha Central American Response Team (OCART). In reality there were three organizations, the above plus Youth for Peace, and their affiliations with national organizations were wider and less well defined. OCART received 'action bulletins' from CISPES, the Nicaragua Network, the Pledge of Resistance (often addressed to "Omaha Pledge of Resistance"), Pax Christi, Witness For Peace (also addressed to an Omaha branch), Medical Aid for El Salvador, and Neighbor to Neighbor (especially concerning their 'coffee boycott'). Activities were coordinated with and information shared with many other national and local groups, especially in the Midwest.[31]

At the same time membership in the three Omaha groups was virtually interchangeable. Although having an established hierarchy with elected officers, each organization was actually what is technically referred to as 'egalitarian' or 'consensual' in structure. They were a 'blob,' a trilobed circle of people with similar political outlooks built around a firm core membership, which threw out tendrils occasionally to draw in new members while losing others from the periphery as enthusiasms waxed and waned. The core membership served as the officers and chief points of contact, while the others gave bulk to demonstrations, letter writing campaigns, petition drives and other programs. This observation tallies with the structure of the Pittsburgh CISPES affiliate, the Central American Mobilization Coalition (CAMC), as reported in an FBI message dated 16 February 1984.

> The membership of CAMC and its affiliated groups appears generally to be of two type groups: the "core" membership and the "affiliate" membership. The "core" membership consists of individuals with strong Communist or Socialist beliefs who have

a history of being active in Communist or Socialist political organizations, some since the Vietnam War era. The "affiliate" membership, on the other hand, consists in large part of local college students relatively new to the political scene. . . . Some of these younger "affiliate" members appear to be politically unsophisticated in that they know little of international current events save what they read or hear at their political meetings. . . . Another group of "affiliate" members consists of older college students, or perhaps graduate students, who appear to have a high degree of political awareness in that they are knowledgeable of world events and are aware of the Communist and U.S. interpretation of these events. These members and affiliates are often members of other groups, such as the Young Socialist, or The Thomas Merton Center.[32]

In OCART this firm core probably numbered around half a dozen people. Minutes of several OCART meetings held in 1990 show only three or four members as being present, who evidently considered this to be enough of a quorum to elect one another to various offices.[33] An undated, computerized OCART mailing list (circa 1990) has fifty-six names on it, while a Youth For Peace phone list has thirty-eight names, with (as expected) some overlap with OCART. It seems apparent that only a tiny fraction of the organization was directly concerned with running it, while the rest were more or less inactive until called upon. This affiliate membership appears to have had a strong college student representation, and many activities occurred in and around Creighton University and at the University of Nebraska at Omaha (UNO).[34] OCART even carried Neighbor to Neighbor's coffee boycott to the UNO cafeteria.[35]

**Responsibility**

Some groups were carefully compartmentalized. One organization, Quixote, had a specialized subgroup dealing with El Salvador called Search For Justice, which was even further specialized in that it dealt specifically with the murder of the six Jesuits during the November 1989 FMLN offensive. It is interesting to note that their 'search for justice' addressed none of the human rights abuses by the FMLN (a general pattern in such groups). A spokesperson was aware of the Zona Rosa killings, characterizing the victims as patrons of a 'ritzy' cafe (perhaps hinting that dining at 'ritzy' cafes makes one a reasonable target for terrorists), but expressed no interest in whether justice was served in this case.[36]

This illustrates another common feature of these groups; selective assumption of responsibility. Many had no 'official' position on the FMLN. Search For Justice was interested only in the Six Jesuits, and if its single-minded pursuit of that issue had unintended consequences, then these obviously were not the organization's fault. Jennifer Jean Casolo's actions during her arrest on November 26, 1989, can be seen as a metaphor for this mindset. When confronted with some of her personal items mixed in with detonator parts, plastic explosive, and AK-47 ammunition, she claimed responsibility for her personal items but "not for the rest of it."[37]

In some groups this bordered on an almost cultish self-delusion. Pax Christi's official position was that it opposed all violence and to sending aid to either side in El Salvador. It claimed that it only protested aid from the U.S. government because that is the only government over which it had any control.[38] Yet it coordinated protest activities with CISPES, an organization clearly the chief FMLN representative in the U.S., called for sending material aid to the FMLN/FDR through SHARE, and endorsed Neighbor to Neighbor's coffee boycott, part of the FMLN's economic disruption campaign.[39] As for it only protesting to its own government, in the fall of 1990 Pax Christi participated with Search For Justice in a coalition activity where petitions were distributed, one version of which was in Spanish. These were to be signed and mailed to 1) the mayor of San Salvador 2) the Salvadoran minister of defense and 3) the President of El Salvador.[40] Why they could not have sent something similar to the Sandinistas, calling for an end to aid to the FMLN, is not really a mystery. Pax Christi's official position was that the FMLN was not receiving aid from the Sandinistas.[41]

**'Peace' Cults**

Contributing to this 'cult' aspect is that many of the groups, such as Quixote, Pax Christi and various 'task forces,' were religious-- based, usually Christian. Some, such as the Maryknolls, were actual

Roman Catholic orders. Their involvement was largely due to the doctrines of liberation theology; a grafting of Marxism onto Christian precepts.

> Coming from Western societies, most foreign "liberation" priests and nuns are even more alien to Latin America's realities than are its own revolutionary leaders, and thus they are even more inclined to avoid a rigorous analysis of the reasons for poverty and passivity by blaming social ills on their own societies. Most or all of these priests and nuns were anticapitalist, antidemocratic, and anti-Western even before they left their countries of origin . . .[42]

Another, perhaps more common, motivation appears to have been what Van Gosse called "instinctual solidarity."[43] This reflexive form of 'solidarity' arose from personal contact with FMLN members and sympathizers through such things as the sanctuary movement, working among the Salvadoran poor, and even deliberate indoctrination.

Many members of these groups were virtually brainwashed through 'educational' programs presenting one-sided (and often erroneous) information, which process appears to have been aided by their misapplication of spiritual faith to secular politics. Faith is necessary in religion, because reason can only go so far in spiritual matters, but its application to Central American issues resulted in serious distortions, including denial of material evidence when this evidence conflicted with FMLN network dogma. The leftist solidarity activists consciously exploited such people for the legitimacy (and the material support) the activists could derive from associating with religious organizations, but appear to have held the latter in contempt for their idealism.

> Despite the persistence of crippling if not chauvinist sentimentality, of illusions of altruism, some element of this instinctual solidarity brings together the 'non-political' sanctuary volunteer in his or her respectable parish with the self-conscious solidarity 'cadre' who reads Omar Cabezas and spends vacations picking Nicaraguan coffee.[44]

The Institute for Food and Development Policy put out a facile justification for 'the ends justify the means' in its *Food First Action*

*Alert* in 1984, which was apparently intended for this audience. This article patiently (and patronizingly) explained how the reader can support violent Marxist revolution in the name of morality; specifically, in the name of the poor.

> We understand the desire of many Americans to avoid endorsing a political process that may not meet all their standards. We hope to show that the responsibility of Americans wanting to ally themselves with the cause of the hungry majority in Central America does not require any compromise of such a principled stance.[45]

**Accountability**

Another serious consideration was these groups' total lack of accountability. Although often arrogating to themselves the title of 'true' representatives of the American people, they were subject to no election and answered to no one outside their own esoteric political circle.[46] For example, a Pledge of Resistance pamphlet trumpeted that "[t]ens of thousands of people" have participated in a nationwide protest, under the banner of "The U.S. People Say No!"[47] How even tens of thousands of people can be considered to be *the* people in a nation of over two hundred million is difficult to grasp. Apparently those involved either elected themselves by acclamation to represent the "U.S. People" without consulting the rest of their presumed constituency, or else they defined themselves as the "U.S. People" in something of a 'Vanguard of the Proletariat' sense, much the same way as they defined the FMLN as the 'Salvadoran People.'[48]

**Double Standards**

As mentioned earlier, although such groups demanded an accounting of U.S. and Salvadoran government actions, they asked nothing of the sort from the FMLN. In his book *How Democracies Perish*, Jean-Francois Revel addressed this issue of double standards.

Besides relating it to the conflict between the East and West, he specifically discussed Central America.

> [D]emocracies were locked of their own free will into an almost insurmountable bind. For they laid down the condition that to have the right to resist absorption into the Communist empire a country must be irreproachably democratic. . . . The trap was a boon to Communist propaganda, which on this point was widely supported by the liberal left in the democracies. And honesty does command that any democrat with consistent ideas deplore the hypocrisy of defending human rights and individual freedom while supporting authoritarian governments. . . .
> And since 1981 we have been assured by the Socialist International and the media in Europe, Latin America and the United States that the West cannot be true to its principles unless it lets El Salvador go totalitarian - unless, of course, it could guarantee simon-pure political, economic, and social democracy there. The general feeling is that only hidebound reactionaries could question the legitimacy of Nicaragua's pretotalitarian, pro-Soviet regime or withhold economic or military aid from it in the name of human rights, political pluralism and democracy.[49]

An example of this double standard is that despite the horror over the 'Contra/CIA Assassination Manual' no comparable moral outrage has arisen over FMLN assassination of Salvadoran officials.[50] A favorite FMLN 'armed propaganda' technique was to kidnap and/or murder local mayors, since they were difficult for the Salvadoran government to protect - also, it should be noted, a favorite Viet Cong tactic.[51] The FMLN was so impressed with this that during late 1988 - early 1989 they threatened most of El Salvador's mayors with death if they didn't resign, then made examples of some who didn't. Nine were murdered and 80 resigned.[52] Remarkably little attention has been paid to this: 'The Six Jesuits' is virtually a slogan (there was even a 60 Minutes segment about it),[53] but 'The Nine Mayors' were somehow forgotten.

## Reform versus Revolution

The focus of official policy was reform, while the focus of the counterpolicy was revolution. Some of the stated, long term objectives of both policy and counterpolicy were quite similar but, besides the problem of definitions (such as of 'democracy'), the means of achieving these goals were quite different. U.S. policy planned to operate within the current framework of society and government by legitimizing the democratic process and strengthening the rule of law, while opponents aimed to sweep it all away and put something new in its place. While CISPES was often coy about its actual goals in its material programmed for release to the general public, other groups, such as the IFDP, openly admitted this orientation.

> Nothing less is required than a fundamental shift in power from a privileged elite to leadership accountable to the majority. Such a genuine shift in power is called "revolution."[54]

This concept of promoting revolution permeates counterpolicy network writings, all the way down to a bumper sticker observed on the back of a Pastors For Peace bus: "BE A REAL REVOLUTIONARY / PRACTICE YOUR FAITH." The word 'reform' was often used, but context proved that something more drastic was really meant. Yet this movement, so deeply involved with an attempt to restructure the society of a foreign country, was opposed in principle to 'intervention.'

### Notes

1. Van Gosse, 14-15.

2. CISPES spokesperson, telephone interview by writer, 22 May 1991.

3. Valerie Richardson, "Salvador rebels promise blood, get cash," *Washington* (D.C.) *Times*, 15 January 1990, NEWSBANK 1990 INT 2:B12.

4. Senate Select Committee on Intelligence, *Senate Select Committee on Intelligence inquiry into the FBI investigation of the Committee in Solidarity with the People of El Salvador (CISPES)*, 101-46, (Washington DC: Government Printing Office, 1989), 67-68.

A particular sticking point for Senator Howard M. Metzenbaum (D-OH) was that he didn't see the connection between CISPES and the CPUSA as proven. He did see that a connection between CISPES and the CPUSA would be significantly damaging to CISPES' claims of innocence. The irony is that proof was already available from an unclassified source. The CPUSA and U.S. Peace Council involvement was confirmed in a biography of Sandy Pollack released by the latter organization in 1986 titled *Sandy Pollack: Her Life*, which described Pollack as a "leading architect of U.S. support for the Salvadoran guerrillas," and a founding member (on the board of directors) of CISPES (Waller, pp. 34-35). She was also on the Permanent Bureau of the World Front For Solidarity with the Salvadoran People (FMSPS) according to its manifesto, as reprinted in Ra'anan, Pfatzgraff, et al, p. 346.

5. Senate 100-1051, 45.

6. S. Steven Powell, *Covert Cadre: Inside the Institute for Policy Studies*, (Ottawa IL: Green Hill Publishers, 1987), 239.

7. Powell, 10.

8. Powell; 24-25, 35, 120-121 & 239.

9. Powell, 229.

10. Father Luis Eduardo Pellecer, phone interview, November 14, 1983, as quoted by Powell, 229.

11. CISPES spokesperson, telephone interview by writer, 12 April 1991.
Ann Butwell (WOLA), during a telephone interview 12 April 1991, suggested that CISPES membership figures were inflated.

12. Angela Sanbrano, Executive Director of CISPES, CISPES action/fundraising letter, circa 1989.

13. Powell, 241.
William H. Kincade and Priscilla B. Hayner, eds., *The ACCESS Resource Guide* (Cambridge MA: Ballinger Publishing Co., 1988), 139-140.

15. Charles Clements, M.D., *Witness To War* (New York: Bantam Books, 1984), 81.

16. Castellanos, 55.

17. Hon. John G. Schmitz, Hon. Fletcher Thompson and Hon. Roger H. Zion, *The Viet Cong Front in the United States*, (Boston: Western Islands), 208.
Reprint of "The Second Front of the Vietnam War: Communist Subversion in the Peace Movement," *Congressional Record*, April 21, 1971.

18. Schmitz, Thompson & Zion, 74-75.

19. Wayman C. Mullins, Ph.D., *Terrorist Organizations in the United States: An Analysis of Issues, Organizations, Tactics and Responses*, (Springfield IL: Charles C. Thomas, 1988), 88.

20. Senate Select Committee on Intelligence, *Senate Select Committee on Intelligence inquiry into the FBI investigation of the Committee in Solidarity with the People of El Salvador (CISPES)*, 100-1051, (Washington DC: Government Printing Office, 1989), 45.

21. Prairie Fire Organizing Committee pamphlet, advertising "an evening of discussion" on El Salvador, featuring "Luis Flores, U.S. Representative, FMLN," at the "New College," on June 9, 1991. A $3.00 donation was called for, to go to the Bravo Fund, which is administered by CISPES. This pamphlet was obtained by the writer mentioning an interest in such an activity during a telephone conversation with the Pledge of Resistance office in Oakland, May 10, 1991.

22. Mullins, 90.

23. Peter Collier & David Horowitz, *Destructive Generation* (New York: Summit Books, 1989), 112.

24. Collier & Horowitz, 112.

25. Jeff Jones, ed., *Brigadista: Harvest and War in Nicaragua* (New York: Praeger Publishers, 1986), Dedication.

26. Powell, 48.

27. Pledge of Resistance, *For Peace in Central America* pamphlet, (Washington DC: Pledge of Resistance National Resource Center, ca. 1990).

28. House 100-42, 36.

29. Ed Asner, fundraising letter for Medical Aid for El Salvador, dated 12 December 1989.

Nicaragua Medical Aid, undated (circa 1989) fundraising letter listing Asner on Advisory board, along with Noam Chomsky, Gus Newport, and Ron Dellums.

Nicaragua Network, *Together For Peace: The Nicaragua Network 1988 Program Report*, (Washington DC: Nicaragua Network, 1988).

30. J. Michael Waller, *The Third Current of Revolution*, (Lanham MD: University Press of America, 1991), 273-274.

Powell, 249-250.

31. Information is from pamphlets and bulletins sent to OCART, which organization allowed the writer to examine its collection of such literature during February-March 1993.

32. House 100-122, 326.

This characterization of the "core" membership as dedicated Communist cadres may be a little harsh to apply to OCART. At least one core OCART member classified himself as a "loyal Democrat" in a Nebraska Peace PAC letter to Representative Peter Hoagland (D-NE), dated October 6, 1990.

33. This does not appear to be unusual in purely volunteer groups, even such formalized organizations as the Civil Air Patrol.

34. Several flyers advertised meeting times at UNO's Milo Bail Student Center for Youth For Peace/UNO, and a January 1990 action bulletin from Pax Christi was addressed to "Youth for Peace, Milo Bail Student Center, Office of Student Activities, UNO, Omaha NE 68182." A flyer dated March 24, 1990 advertising a "March to End U.S. War in El Salvador" named Degelman Circle on the Creighton campus as the assembly point.

35. Youth for Peace-UNO letter to UNO Food Service, November 7, 1990.

This was in accordance with Neighbor to Neighbor's *Salvadoran Coffee Boycott Action Guide - Spring 1990* (San Francisco: Neighbor to Neighbor, 1990), 4.

36. Maureen Fiedler, QUIXOTE Center, telephone interview by writer, 17 April 1991.

37. Jennifer Jean Casolo, videotape of her arrest released by National Police of El Salvador, 26 November 1989.
This film was actually shot the night of the 25th: she was arrested the next day. In part of it she is standing in the back yard, next to piles of ordinance, while digging continues. She later denied being allowed into the back yard during the digging and stated during television interviews that she was being framed by the Salvadoran government, which "planted" the evidence. Precisely how they could have planted so much without anyone noticing was never explained. Many other inconsistencies in her story were overlooked during these interviews.

38. Pax Christi spokesperson Sister Marlene Bertke, telephone interview 15 February 1993.

39. Pax Christi letter, circa January 1990.

40. Search for Justice, "Petition to the High Command of the Salvadoran Military," October/November 1990.

41. Sister Marlene Bertke, Pax Christi spokesperson, telephone interview 15 February 1993.

42. Michael Radu, "Revolutionary Elites," *Violence and the Latin American Revolutionaries*, ed. Michael Radu (New Brunswick NJ: Transaction Books, 1988), 118.

43. Van Gosse, 15.

44. Van Gosse, 15.

45. "Nicaragua: Give Change a Chance," *Food First Action Alert* (Institute for Food and Development Policy, 1984), 1.

46. Clements, 138.
Ken Butigan, *The U.S. People Say NO: Nationwide Protest of U.S. Policy in El Salvador*, (Pledge of Resistance, 1989); and numerous other pamphlets, newsletters, articles, etc. by FMLN support network organizations.

47. Ken Butigan, *The U.S. People Say NO: Nationwide Protest of U.S. Policy in El Salvador*, (Pledge of Resistance, 1989).

48. Paul Duggan, "D.C. Demonstrators Protest El Salvador Election," *The Washington Post*, 20 March 1989, A27.

49. Jean-Francois Revel, *How Democracies Perish* (New York: Harper & Row, 1983), 295-296.

50. *Psychological Operations in Guerrilla Warfare*, with essays by Joanne Omang & Aryeh Neier (New York: Vintage Books, 1985).
Neither has there been any condemnation of Che Guevara's *Guerrilla Warfare*, which specifically addresses the pros & cons and tactical use of political assassination. The 'assassination manual' refers only to "neutralizing" officials. It should also be noted that both Omang and Neier were associated with IPS activities - Omang had taught courses at IPS, and Neier headed IPS spinoff Americas Watch at a time when that organization was sycophantically pro-Sandinista.

51. Chris Norton, "Massive resignation of Salvadoran mayors undercuts U.S. strategy," *Latinamerica Press*, 26 January 1989, 1.
Chris Norton was closely associated with the Salvadoran labor union FENA-STRAS, a member organization in the DRU. This information also appears on the front page of the February 1989 issue of *FOCUS*, a newsletter published by the Intercommunity Center for Justice and Peace. The *Latinamerica Press* and *FOCUS* were distributed widely through the FMLN support networks, which means that members of these networks were aware of (at least) this FMLN political assassination program.

52. Morton M. Kondracke, "Salvador's Silver Lining," *The New Republic*, 13 March 1989, 24.
Actually, Mr. Kondracke states "nine mayors and one governor." The U.N. Truth Commission put the number at ten.

53. CBS News-60 Minutes Public Relations, telephone interview by writer, 21 May 1991.
Spokesperson confirmed that segments had never been produced on the Zona Rosa killings. The FMLN terror campaign against Salvadoran mayors was not discussed during the segment on the 16 November 1989 murder of the six Jesuits.

54. "Nicaragua: Give Change a Chance," 1.
This "leadership accountable to the majority" sounds good, but in this case refers to the Sandinistas. To the IFDP Castro was another leader "accountable to the majority" and in El Salvador it would have referred to the FMLN.

## Chapter 6

# War of Information

What is the difference, really, if the organization attempting to influence another nation's internal affairs is a private or official one? Surely, attempting to impose one's own agenda on the politics of a foreign country is just as much an intervention as if it was being done by the CIA. If it was immoral to attempt to export U.S.-style democracy because of its alienness to Central America, then how could it be more moral to install equally alien Marxism? The argument that the FMLN/FDR truly represented the people of El Salvador because it was a Salvadoran organization composed of Salvadorans is nullified by the fact that ARENA had the same qualifications. Additionally, ARENA was willing to participate in the democratic process, to which the FMLN was violently opposed. Using Western democratic guidelines, which organization seems more legitimate?

William Walker intruded into a Nicaraguan civil war on the invitation of the 'Democratic' (Liberal) Party, which was fighting the Conservatives (also known as 'Legitimists'). He and his men were private citizens, soldiers of fortune called 'filibusters.'[1] Thus organizations which took an active part in the Salvadoran civil war - whether by supporting the FMLN or merely by opposing the elected government - can justifiably be seen as modern filibusters.

A prime example of this type of intervention was CISPES' use of propaganda. CISPES and the other pro-FMLN groups were a small, "electorally insignificant"[2] minority in the United States, who managed to have an exaggerated effect on U.S. public perceptions of the war in El Salvador, and thus (through this effect on U.S. domestic politics) an even more exaggerated effect on internal Salvadoran politics.[3] Taking their lessons from the Vietnam War, they used a variety of methods to disseminate the FMLN's party line and attempt to discredit opposing viewpoints. This campaign was far more than merely providing moral support. It was integrated into the FMLN's strategy for prosecuting the war, and although the main thrust was to have all U.S. aid cut off, portions of the program can be clearly linked with specific FMLN objectives.

**Demonstrations**

Demonstrations are one of the most popular techniques by which a tiny minority can get its opinions widely disseminated, and were extensively used by the FMLN networks. These were carefully organized and were usually a 'coalition activity' of some sort. Influencing the news media was considered to be especially important. One example was generated by the murder of the Six Jesuits.

A 1989 Pledge of Resistance pamphlet lists 370 protest activities from November 13 to December 18, 1989. Activities included painting 'white hands' (after the Salvadoran 'Mano Blanco' death squads) on the Federal Building in San Francisco, an assortment of 'die-ins,' a tableau of dummies to represent the Six Jesuits, chalking outlines to represent the Six Jesuits, memorial services for the Six Jesuits, 'bannering,' fasting, and a great deal of deliberate 'civil disobedience.' Examples of the last included blockades of Federal offices, deliberate trespassing, and occupation of Congressional offices.

This pamphlet goes on to claim that "1452 people have been arrested engaging in civil disobedience, while 989 others have risked arrest . . . This office has documented 412 demonstrations, . . . These activities have been organized by the Pledge of Resistance and a wide number of organizations and their local groups, including CISPES, Witness for Peace, and Quest for Peace."[4]

Another example comes from a CISPES fundraising letter signed by Angela Sanbrano, undated but probably sent out in 1989. Its focus is the 1988 elections and CISPES' efforts to break what it called a 'media blockade.'

> We also have proved we can keep the media's eye on El Salvador. Last year, when the Death Squads were a non-issue in the U.S. presidential campaign, CISPES broke the media blockade. We put up signs in buses and subways in major U.S. cities calling for "No U.S. $$ to the Death Squad Government in El Salvador." And our community organizing resulted in protests in over a 100 cities, culminating in a Pentagon protest just prior to the U.S. presidential elections. The results: nationwide TV coverage and editorials in major U.S. dailies urging our government to pull out of El Salvador.[5]

The letter went on to boast of a "demonstration held at the State Department in Washington, D.C., which was carried on all three major networks." And how Michael Lent (listed as Organizational Director) appeared on "ABC's Nightline, with millions of Americans watching." Additionally, Sanbrano discussed CISPES 'Action Networks.'

> CISPES' grassroots Action Networks of tens of thousands of people are on the alert to do whatever is necessary in the event the army Death Squads kill opposition leaders or the U.S. escalates the war. That includes flooding the White House with telegrams, or Congress with phone calls, or organizing nonviolent grassroots protest in hundreds of cities across the U.S.[6]

These action networks were found throughout the movement, and were activated by 'action bulletins' or something similarly named.[7] These bulletins, as implied above, covered specific issues and called for specific action. Often a printed form was included, sometimes to be read over the telephone, sometimes to be signed and sent as a letter, telegram, or petition. Some were more long-term, containing a calendar of suggested events and lists (with telephone numbers and addresses) of whom to coordinate them with and against. As an interesting variation requiring the least amount of effort from the protester, there were postcards with a message on one side and the general address for the House of Representatives or the Senate on the other. The recipient simply signed it, wrote his or her Congressman's name in the blank above the address, and mailed it.

Some of these action messages had an operational slant, and were apparently intended to cripple some specific Salvadoran military capability which was doing damage to the FMLN at that point. For example, the Salvadoran Air Force became increasingly effective against the rebels during the mid 1980s, and this was reflected in CISPES propaganda.

> In civilian areas like Chalatenango, El Salvador, U.S.-supplied planes indiscriminately bomb three or four times daily, in what can only be called acts of premeditated murder. I've been told that, as the U.S.-trained pilots seek their targets, women in colorful dresses must take cover lest they draw fire.[8]

At the time, the northeastern part of Chalatenango was what the FMLN liked to call a 'liberated zone,' dominated by the Popular Liberation Forces (FPL) faction of the FMLN.[9] As an area where the FMLN operated in force it was indeed bombed, sometimes several times a day, by the Salvadoran Air Force while supporting Army operations against FPL units. It is no coincidence that Sanbrano was so concerned about Chalatenango; of the five FMLN tendencies, CISPES' closest relations were with the FPL.[10] There is no evidence to support the accusation that the Salvadoran pilots were deliberately targeting brightly dressed women, and this story appears to be fabricated atrocity along the lines of the ludicrous World War I propaganda of 'Huns' eating French babies.

These examples also reveal some of the characteristic inconsistencies of the movement. Clearly, they had no particular aversion to breaking the law to get their point across, nor to harassing those with whom they disagreed.[11] This is particularly significant in light of their condemnation of U.S. policy as 'illegal and immoral,' their accusations of 'illegal FBI harassment,' and their acute, almost hysterical, sensitivity to both criticism and any hint of outside examination of their activities.[12] Another prominent inconsistency is that although they demanded 'the truth' about Central America, and called some of their programs 'educational,' many of their accepted 'facts' were actually quite dubious, and their "educational" material was blatantly one-sided and often untrue.[13]

**Disinformation: The School of the Americas**

One form of propaganda is disinformation. That is, distorting the truth, often by using part of it to lead into a lie. One example comes from a pamphlet on the U.S. Army's School of the Americas (SOA) put out by SOA Watch, a CISPES operation directed against the training of Salvadoran troops at Fort Benning, Georgia.[14] The first part of the pamphlet, titled "Schooling in Hatred," describes the murder of the Six Jesuits' housekeeper and daughter in some detail, then goes on to reveal that "according to documentation provided to Rep. Joseph Moakley's Task Force by the U.S. Assistant Secretary of Defense," the murderers had been trained at Ft. Benning. In the subsequent section titled "What Kind of training do Salvadoran soldiers receive?" it claims that the Army refused to divulge how foreign students were trained in human rights issues, but that one of the buildings had a sign which read (in Spanish) "Classroom for Low Intensity Conflict." It then 'defines' Low Intensity Conflict.

> The war strategy known as Low Intensity Conflict targets anyone advocating change in El Salvador's impoverished and unjust society as a "subversive" or "communist." Priests, teachers, health care workers, union leaders, cooperative members, human rights advocates and catechists are among its victims. Since 1980, over 73,000 people [sic] have been killed in El Salvador's Low Intensity Conflict war.[15]

This definition is not supported by anything in the pamphlet nor by any objective evidence.[16] The train of logic derails in the preceding paragraph with the insinuation that anyone trained in Low Intensity Warfare is necessarily trained to commit atrocities. By this same logic, with Charles Clements as an example, it can be insinuated that anyone trained at the Air Force Academy must become a conscientious objector and an active supporter of the FMLN! The basic premise of the pamphlet is a lie, supported by verifiable - but irrelevant - facts manipulated with twisted logic. This pattern was consistently repeated in CISPES (and other FMLN support network) literature.

## Disinformation: Soviet Bloc Support for the FMLN

One of the 'big lies' of the war was the minimizing, or outright denial, of the fact of Soviet, Cuban, and Sandinista military support for the FMLN. This is still widely accepted, despite documentation, testimony, and literally tons of material evidence to the contrary. It appears in Phillip Berryman's Inside Central America, beginning, ironically, a page after Berryman supports his own views with the infamous November 6 1980 State Department 'Dissent Memo,' since shown to have been a KGB forgery.[17]

> Scarcely a month after the inauguration, the Reagan administration produced a white paper that claimed, on the basis of allegedly captured guerrilla documents, that arms were being shipped from Soviet-bloc countries through Cuba and Nicaragua to Salvadoran rebels. This white paper was subsequently shown to be based on unjustified extrapolations, false readings and translations, and quite possibly, forged documents.[18]

In fact, much of the information in this white paper - as in so many other documents 'discredited' by the left - has been supported by other sources. Berryman himself offers no evidence for his assertions, and qualifies his accusation that the documents were forged with "quite possibly." Examination of the captured papers reveals the translations to be reasonable, and the "unjustified extrapolations" and "false readings" to fall in line with what has been discovered about the FMLN's arms pipeline.[19]

Charles Clements, in *Witness to War*, provided more examples of this disinformation. He did this two ways. One was by creating a spurious 'straw man' - equating 'support' with actual Soviet, Cuban, and Nicaraguan combatants in the field - and demolishing it by saying that he never saw any.[20] Another was by claiming that all the weapons used by the guerrillas were captured or purchased, and none came in as Soviet-bloc aid.[21] This was patently untrue.

Figure 3. *Oxfam-owned VW van used to smuggle arms and documents to the FMLN.*

The arms flow from Nicaragua to El Salvador was carried out by sea, land and air, with the last component being the least important by tonnage carried. The sea 'corridor' was managed by the ERP, and used ocean-going canoes, or *cayucos*, from Chinandega, Nicaragua, across the Gulf of Fonseca and up to the Usulutan coast.[22] Salvadoran surveillance and interdiction of this route became more effective in the mid-1980s, due primarily to the deployment of the U.S. Navy SEAL-trained 'Barracuda' and Piranha' naval commando units to La Union. According to one source, in an attempt to counter this effort mother ships came into use, unloading onto *cayucos* off the northern coast.[23]

The land route through Honduras was used from the beginning, and became more important as problems arose with the sea route. This method utilized modified vehicles, mostly vans and tractor-trailer trucks, with hollows packed with supplies. Several such vehicles were captured, but this method remained a favorite throughout the war and became more important as sea delivery became more difficult.[24]

A clear example of the international FMLN support network's participation in this arms smuggling effort was provided when a Volkswagen van driven by a French national was stopped by Honduran authorities on 27 August 1990. The van contained 229 stabilizing fins, "ignition charges," propellant increments and 4 firing data tables for 81mm mortars, plus FMLN documents.[25] The van was owned by a 'humanitarian' organization called Oxfam-Belgium and was supposed to be employed in Nicaragua on project "NIC/0000," with Stefan Declerq listed as the consignee.[26] According to the driver, Eve Demaziere (or Demassiere), it was her sixth smuggling run.[27]

Figure 5. *Wreckage of a Nicaraguan Cessna 310 which crashed in El Salvador on 25 November 1989.*

Participation in arms smuggling by U.S. based networks is suggested by the recovery of three Chinese assault rifles and large amounts of Chinese-made ammunition in FMLN arms caches during the 1989 offensive. The rifles were semiautomatic copies of the AK-47 in 5.56mm NATO caliber, with serial numbers that proved them to have been sold in Dallas, Texas. In a probable attempt to disguise its origin, the ammunition had all been removed from its original boxes, but the headstamps were all from batches made by the PRC exclusively for the United States commercial market.[28]

The air 'corridor' was earlier controlled by the FPL, but this operation was shut down when the FPL's Costa Rican mercenary pilot was arrested on 25 January 1981.[29] After 1981 airlift seems to have been used primarily for high priority items, as evidenced by the

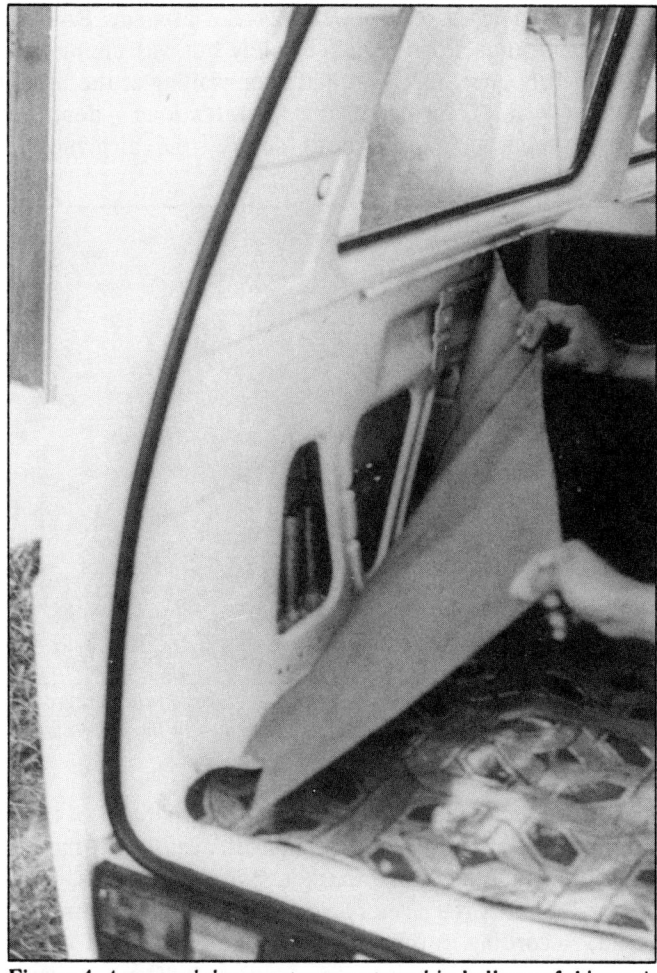

**Figure 4.** *Arms and documents were stowed in hollows of this van's body. Tractor-trailer trucks were usually specially modified.*

two Nicaraguan aircraft loaded with anti-aircraft missiles which were lost in El Salvador on 25 November 1989, during the FMLN offensive.[30] Subsequent investigation points to their having taken off from an airstrip at Montelimar in Nicaragua, and to have been part of a Sandinista operation called "Plan Mariposa."[31] One, a Cessna 310, crashed on landing in El Salvador. Three crewmembers died in the crash, while a fourth crawled from the wreckage and committed suicide. Included in its cargo were 24 Soviet-made SA-7 *Strela* missiles.[32] The other aircraft landed safely but was unable to take off again. FMLN guerrillas, who had been waiting at the little-used airstrip for two days, carted off the aircraft's load - described as "long green tubes" - and tried to destroy the airplane before abandoning it.[33]

Figure 6. *Nicaraguan Cessna's cargo. The tubes in the foreground hold Soviet-made Strela (SA-7) missiles. Bodies of the crew can be seen at left center.*

Miguel Castellanos stated that "[b]y 1983, 60 percent of the arms came from the exterior, and 30 percent were acquired by the FMLN by requisition and the black market."[34] By his figures, only ten percent of the FMLN's armory was obtained by capture on the battlefield. According to official figures, the Salvadoran Army suffered a net loss of 1277 rifles from January 1981 to August 1984, which would only have equipped 12-15% of the FMLN's guerrillas at that time.[35] Included in these losses would be an indeterminate number (probably most) of the weapons actually sold on the black market, since loss in combat would be the safest way to report them to higher authorities.

'Western' or 'capitalist' weapons were deliberately sought by the FMLN, apparently to support this disinformation campaign.[36] In the early 1980's the FMLN was equipped largely with M-16's - many from Vietnam - and FN FAL's (including a number from Cuba with the telltale Cuban crest drilled out).[37] This was at a time when the Salvadoran Army was equipped with G-3 rifles, and M-16's were just coming into service with some elite units.[38] Besides Vietnam and Cuba, the FMLN was able to get 'capitalist' weapons from Ethiopia and through a 'triangular deal' with Nicaragua. In the last case, Sandinista Popular Army (EPS) stocks of National Guard weapons were passed to the FMLN and replaced with new Soviet bloc equipment.[39] This is probably where many Israeli-made Galil rifles, which appeared in captured FMLN shipping documents and in the hands of elite FMLN troops in El Salvador, came from.[40]

There is also the matter of unique weapons obviously not obtained from the El Salvadoran military or even the international arms trade. In 1988 a grenade launcher was captured from the guerrillas during an attack. It was a 'pump action' repeater apparently built around a barrel from the helicopter mounted version of the Soviet AG-17 automatic grenade launcher, and firing a "30mm VOG-17M HE/fragmentation grenade normally launched by the Plamya, which exists in a ground tripod-mounted version and in an airborne one arming Mi-8 Hip helicopters...." Provenance of this and similar weapons have never been reliably established, but both Cuba and the Sandinistas were known to have had both the AGS-17 Plamya and Mil Mi-8 on inventory at the time.[41]

The pretense of self-sufficiency was decisively shattered by the 1989 offensive, when the FMLN took the field openly equipped with Soviet bloc weapons.[42] The transportation and stockpiling of these weapons in preparation for the offensive apparently took at least a year, despite FMLN propaganda that the offensive was a spontaneous reaction provoked by rightist attacks on FMLN-associated labor unions. For example, on 31 May 1989 an arms cache described as the largest uncovered since the beginning of the war was discovered in a lumberyard in San Salvador. It contained "283 Soviet Bloc AK-47 assault rifles, hundreds of thousands of rounds of Cuban-made ammunition made in 1988, 892 blocks of TNT explosives, grenade launchers, sophisticated timers and other materiel."[43] On 19 October 1989, barely a month before the offensive, a truck bound for San Salvador was stopped in Honduras and found to contain what was described at the time as a "record shipment of weapons."

> A preliminary search of the truck found 307 rocket-propelled grenades and an undetermined number of launchers; 74 automatic rifles, including AK-47s and M-16s with an undetermined amount of ammunition; explosive detonators, radios and urban guerrilla training manuals with "FMLN" stamped on them . . .[44]

## Disinformation: The Death Toll

Another piece of disinformation concerns the number of people killed in the war, and who is to blame for their deaths. A prepared statement by Reverend Gregory S. Brown dated 19 February 1987, stated that the "civil war in El Salvador . . . has killed over 62,000 civilians in the last seven years."[45] During the 1989 FMLN offensive, one supporter went somewhat farther.

> At a Tuesday vigil at noon on the steps of the U.S. Capitol, the Rev. Joe Mulligan, a Jesuit priest who works in Nicaragua, decried the "massive bombing" carried out by the U.S. trained Salvadoran army. "How many other heads have been blown off? . . . Hundreds of thousands of heads," said Father Mulligan, who works with the Central American Historical Institute, a pro-Sandinista organization in Managua. "We must insist on a cutoff of military aid to the government," Father Mulligan said.[46]

In recent CISPES propaganda the count has been more moderate, varying from 70,000 to 75,000, and the inference is that they were all civilians murdered by the 'death squad' Salvadoran government with massive U.S. assistance.[47] These last figures have been widely accepted, but where did they really come from?

> In the absence of hard figures, reporters and human rights observers were left to their own devices. Having nothing more than death rates in previous years as a yardstick, by the mid-eighties the practice of simply adding 5,000 or more dead a year to the total became a habit. . . .
> In some cases "mortality inflation" was completely intentional. During a January 1991 dinner party, two reporters, [names deleted], joked to emboffs [embassy officers] that, in journalist circles, it was a real badge of honor to get one's newspaper to print a

new, higher body count figure. After giving all due credit to the fellow journalist who had recently gotten the figure hiked from 70,000 to 75,000, the two reporters quipped that there had not, of course, been anything near 5,000 more fatalities since the figure was last upped, from 65,000 to 70,000, but noted that the figures bandied about by the press had long ceased to have any basis in reality. Once one newspaper printed a higher figure - and the game among journalists covering El Salvador was to get the figure boosted by 5,000 every six months, regardless of what was happening on the ground - all the other newspapers followed suit in using the new, inflated toll, the reporters explained.[48]

It thus appears that the most widely accepted statistics on the war were simply made up. A more reasonable total figure, derived from a minimum amount of documentation and study, would be 65,000. This is based on the Americas Watch estimate of the civilian toll as 40,000,[49] plus an estimate of combatants killed in action as around 25,000. To detail the latter, according to the U.S. State Department and the Salvadoran Army respectively, 6,335/9,140 soldiers were killed, while the FMLN lost 16,075/23,480.[50] Americas Watch offered no figures on combat deaths but suggested that the Salvadoran Army's 'body count' was inflated, so going with the high number of government troops and the low number of guerrillas, we get a total of 25,215.[51]

This 65,000 figure is probably close to the total violent deaths during the war, but as an actual toll of the war it is likely to be high. A 1992 U.S. Embassy study cautiously gives a 'floor number' of 26,708 civilian war dead, suggesting that the actual count may be 10,000 or so higher. However, the study also states that much common crime was probably disguised by the chaos, especially in the very early 1980s.

> At the outset of the conflict, it was not unusual for as many as 100 bodies of victims of political violence to be discovered in a single morning. During the conflict, many Salvadorans hid common crime and settled personal vendettas under the guise of political violence. The number of such killings will never be known.[52]

Americas Watch apparently considered ordinary criminal murder to comprise an insignificant proportion of the total killed in El Salvador, and used circumstantial evidence to decide whether a murder was political or not, and, if apparently political, which side carried it out. For example, if union leaders were found murdered execution style, then it was assumed that a right-wing death squad had done it.[53]

There are several problems with this approach. For one thing, criminal murder was not an insignificant factor, and cannot be reliably separated from political murder if the perpetrators and their motives are not positively identified. There has long been a high 'ambient level' of violence in Central America. Five years before the war, in 1974, murder was the fourth leading cause of death in El Salvador, and the overall murder rate was 33.0 per 100,000 population (actually down slightly from 1968, when it was 38.0). For males the rate was even higher, being 62.5![54] By applying these rates to the average population of El Salvador during the period (4.8 million), the expectation becomes that even in 'normal' times about 20,000 people would be murdered from 1979 to 1992. This is putting aside for the moment the reasonable assumption that during times of great social stress the rate would go up. Obviously, ordinary criminal murder was not an insignificant factor. And the Americas Watch technique of relying on circumstantial evidence appears to be vulnerable to being exploited in order to disguise such crime as political terrorism. The indicators used to determine political murder were not, by any means, secret.

If the Americas Watch criteria could be exploited by ordinary criminals (and statistically it appears that they were), then it is equally possible that they could be used to disguise FMLN political murders. In several cases FMLN death squads wore Army uniforms, and even on occasion identified themselves as "the authorities."[55] This has been documented only because the killers took credit afterwards. There have been persistent allegations that the FMLN also did this without taking credit for it later, or even blaming the Salvadoran security forces for the action.[56] That they could have done so is well within the bounds of probability. Just such an assassination was committed in Managua in 1983. Dr. Melida Anaya Montes (Commandante Ana Maria) was stabbed eighty-three times with an icepick, and then her throat was cut. The killers were tracked down by the Sandinista police, who publicly announced that they expected to find a "CIA commando" of some sort. Instead they caught 'Marcelo' of the FMLN, who had murdered Dr. Montes on orders from Cayetanio Carpio (Commandante General Marcial) as part of an ideological dispute, and tried to cover it up by framing the CIA.[57]

| Year | Tutela Legal | U.S. Embassy |
|---|---|---|
| 1980 | 12-15,000 | 11,000 |
| 1981 | 12-15,000 | 10,000 |
| 1982 | 5,339 | 6,000 |
| 1983 | 5,142 | 7,682 |
| 1984 | 2,024 | 4,360 |
| 1985 | | 1,892 |
| 1986 | | 1,736 |
| 1987 | | 1,858 |
| 1988 | | 1,639 |
| 1989 | | 3,403 |
| 1990 | | 2,266 |
| 1991 | | 1,982 |

Table 1. *Total violent deaths in El Salvador, 1980-1991. Figures released by* Tutela Legal, *the Catholic human rights monitoring group, support the idea of a decrease in killings of all kinds after 1981, with a sharp dropoff after 1983. It appears that most of those killed in the war died during the period 1980-1983.* Tutela Legal *stopped estimating yearly totals in 1984, but Embassy figures for the rest of the 1980s show deaths subsiding to something close to the prewar murder rate. This is confirmed by* Statistical Abstract of Latin America, Vol. 29 *figures (p. 153, table 718) showing a violent death rate of 40.7 (still the 4th ranked cause of death) for 1984. This reduced yearly toll was doubled in 1989 due to the*

*FMLN offensive.* (From *Salvadoran Deaths Due to War 1980- -1991*, 26 March 1992.)

Another case comes from *Witness to War*. A guerrilla *sanitario* (medical assistant) named Mario was 'tried' as a traitor and executed.[58] The only way anyone knows the man was killed by the FMLN is from Dr. Clements' book. Had Americas Watch investigated (and they may have), they would have found a known FMLN member shot to death at close range and buried in a shallow grave. By their methods, and unless the FMLN corrected them (not very likely), they would have chalked him up as another victim of the death squads.

A large component of the civilian casualties came from people caught in the crossfire between rebel and government forces. During the November 1989 offensive the FMLN entrenched itself in heavily populated neighborhoods, and forced the residents to work for them at gunpoint, using them as a 'living shield.'[59] As a result about a thousand civilians were killed in this action alone.[60] The remarkably well coordinated reaction to these casualties by CISPES arouses suspicions that the FMLN deliberately engineered them in order to make useful propaganda for their support networks abroad.[61] Considering the FMLN's casual attitude towards collateral damage, evidenced by the nine bystanders they killed while machine-gunning the four unarmed U.S. Marines in 1985, this is entirely possible.

There is also the problem of determining which casualties were civilian noncombatants and which were guerrillas in mufti. This is a significant problem of anti-guerrilla warfare in general. Killing noncombatants deliberately is a crime, but killing combatants is, of course, not. But just how do you identify 'combatants?' In published photographs often the only distinction was that the guerrillas were armed.[62] In *Witness to War* a 61 year old man leaning on an FAL assault rifle is presented as "Guazapa's oldest combatant," while directly across from him a young woman with a Madsen submachine gun slung at her side and a baby in her arms is identified as "A Guazapa guerrilla holding up her infant."[63] Both are in civilian clothes. If they were killed in combat one suspects that 'human rights' observers would consider them civilian noncombatants, and the presence of weapons and other military equipment (if they were left with the bodies) as window dressing for a coverup of a Salvado-

**Figure 7.** *A youthful FMLN combatant armed with an M-16.*

ran Army 'massacre.'

Due to these factors it appears likely that the Americas Watch estimate of 40,000 civilian 'war' dead is an inflated figure. It is tempting to arbitrarily subtract the 20,000 expected murder toll from this total, but due to the many variables and inconsistencies in the available statistics something between 10,000 and 20,000 seems to be more reasonable. The resultant 20,000 to 30,000 is still a guess, but at least one based on available documentation. It is also less than a third to less than a half of CISPES' 75,000 figure.

It thus seems clear that the figures tossed around by CISPES were not reliable, and that actual terrorist murders - done with a political objective in mind - were far fewer than CISPES would have us believe. To which must be added, of these murders an uncertain percentage were committed by the FMLN. Adding this to the assertions by the U.S. State Department and the Salvadoran government that right-wing terrorism was sharply curbed by 1983 - assertions supported by figures released by Tutela Legal - and it becomes theoretically possible that by the end of the war the leftists equalled (or even exceeded) the rightists in directed killings of civilians for political purposes.

The consensus is still, however, that over the course of the war the right-wing death squads killed more than the leftist ones. The next question to be answered is: were these rightist death squads really working for the Salvadoran government? Although it is undoubted that members of the security forces and ARENA did engage in political killings, there is no real basis for the charge that the 'death squads' were part of Salvadoran government policy, as was asserted in (among other sources) Amnesty International's 1988 report *"Death Squads" - A Government Strategy*. As Schwartz cautions, "Amnesty International does itself a disservice by asserting as fact that which is only informed speculation."[64]

The National Republican Alliance (ARENA), despite the leading role of Roberto D'Aubuisson, was not really a 'death squad' either. That many individuals, even party officials, have been involved with the death squads has been fairly well proven.[65] But convincing evidence that the party itself was organized in order to carry out such a campaign is lacking, and the vast majority of the party's members and supporters seemed content to work within the political system. (The same, of course, cannot be said of the FMLN/FDR.)[66] The violently inclined tended to have parallel membership in a "rightist vigilante organization," such as the Secret Anti-Communist Army (ESA), Maximiliano Hernandez Brigade, or the Organization for Liberation from Communism (OLC).[67]

## Indoctrination as Entertainment

Hollywood was especially helpful in the propaganda effort. Much as the *New York World* inflamed American public opinion against the Spanish rule of Cuba at the turn of the century with: "Blood on the roadsides, blood in the fields, blood on the doorsteps, blood, blood, blood,"[68] movies such as *Salvador* and *Romero* presented the FMLN party line in wide-screen technicolor. A more indirect approach was made on the television program "V", which made frequent favorable references to the Salvadoran guerrillas, and finally advanced to directly comparing its fictional characters' resistance against lizard-like alien invaders with the war in El Salvador. It doesn't take much perspicacity to guess who the reptiles were supposed to be.

Besides such disguised propaganda, Hollywood celebrities were involved with a number of 'documentaries' put out by the FMLN networks. One fairly typical example was Neighbor to Neighbor's *Faces of War*, which featured Mike Farrell of *MASH* fame. This film, as its title implies, concentrated on emotive scenes - particularly limpid-eyed children playing in front of, or giggling at, the camera - at the expense of facts. The information presented was biased, unverifiable, or untrue.

A clear example of bias was that although the film was dated 1986, the 1980 murder of the four churchwomen was emphasized, while the 1985 'Zona Rosa massacre' of four Marines and nine bystanders was not even mentioned. This lack is particularly telling since N2N's comparison of El Salvador with the Vietnam War concentrated on the Memorial, with its long list of the dead, and the implication that continued U.S. involvement in El Salvador would inevitably lead to the same. (Not surprisingly, this was one of the FMLN's pet propaganda approaches as well.)[69] Senator Christopher Dodd was featured in this section, speaking solemnly of the "dark tunnel of endless intervention." It appears that the filmmakers intended to raise the specter of massive U.S. casualties as the cost of intervention, but at the same time didn't want to broadcast the fact that the FMLN was killing Americans.

The dollar amounts of U.S. aid to El Salvador, given with a straight face by Mr. Farrell, were incorrect. A $3 billion total was mentioned, with the clear implication that none of it was for food, and most (later presented as half, or about $1.5 billion) was intended for weapons. According to verifiable statistics, total U.S. aid to El Salvador from 1970 to 1986 (including loans) was $2.3 billion. Of this, $1.6 billion was economic aid (of which $290 million was specifically food aid) and $665 million (less than half of N2N's figure) was for military purposes.[70] To compare, from 1979 to 1983 Nicaragua received $2.3 billion in loans *alone* from various sources.[71]

The film also condemned the Nicaraguan Resistance (part of the general pattern - pro-FMLN/anti-Contra), and there was an interesting reference to a town named Wiwili in Nicaragua. A bride was shown weeping over her groom, killed by the contras on the woman's wedding day. The interesting part is that mass graves of victims of the Sandinista secret police (DGSE) have been uncovered near Wiwili.[72] Since contras historically tended to operate near their old homes, and were often campesinos who had been victimized by the Sandinistas, it is possible that this 'atrocity' was in fact a revenge killing. N2N did not provide enough information about the victim to confirm this hypothesis, but their oddly sketchy treatment of the victim - most other people in the film were much more fully identified, especially politically - leaves room for speculation.

**The Coffee Boycott**

Another of Neighbor to Neighbor's projects was the 'Coffee Boycott,' which is an excellent example of direct participation by the U.S. support networks in a declared FMLN program. According to Neighbor to Neighbor it had - officially - no position on the FMLN.[73] However, it did have an obvious hostility towards the elected government of El Salvador, and this 'official position' appears to have been formulated in order to plausibly deny the actual focus of its operations. The FMLN/FDR connection is proved by N2N's own *Action Guide*, which stated that the FMLN-controlled National Union of Salvadoran Workers (UNTS) and Federation of Associations of Cooperatives (COACES) had endorsed the boycott.[74]

Coffee is El Salvador's leading export.[75] It was also an important target in the FMLN's economic disruption campaign.[76] Ostensibly the coffee boycott was designed to help the people of El Salvador by bringing the '14 Families' who control the government, oppress the workers, etc. to their knees.[77]

> The "fourteen families" are the small group of coffee plantation owners who have dominated El Salvador's political and economic life for generations. With the profits from coffee exports, they promote death squads, prevent reform, and block a negotiated settlement to the war.[78]

The '14 Families' are a myth. As a symbol of the planter elite this myth has some relevance, but the second sentence of the quotation twists it into fantasy. The reality was 8,867 families of coffee growers, 183,000 directly employed workers, and over 500,000 indirectly employed workers.[79] It is possible that some coffee growers participated in death squad activities, but this blanket condemnation of a whole industry is completely unsupported by objective evidence. Besides the traditional coffee planting families, many of the growers got their start in the 'Land to the Tiller' and similar agrarian reform programs. Twenty-two collective farms were operating as part of these programs.[80] N2N denied to its members that the smaller growers would be hurt by the boycott, but this rationale makes no sense unless the boycott as a whole was completely ineffective.[81] For one thing, N2N made no distinction between coffee grown by small operations and that by larger ones; it called for a total boycott of Salvadoran coffee. For another, neither Incafe (the government agency - formerly a monopoly - which handled much of the foreign coffee sales) nor the coffee companies graded coffee by the size of the operation growing it.[82] Coffee was (and is) graded by quality.

Among the techniques employed in the campaign were the usual letter writing and telephone calls, but this time much of the pressure was applied to a private company; the Folger's Coffee subsidiary of Procter & Gamble. The strategy behind the campaign against Folger's is revealed in a pamphlet put out by the Chicago branch of N2N around 1990.

> Right now the boycott is focused on Folger's because it's the largest U.S. brand. If we can force Folger's, which is owned by

Procter and Gamble, to stop buying Salvadoran coffee, this alone will cause a tremendous drop in Salvadoran coffee sales. Then we can concentrate on Nestle and General Foods, the other big U.S. coffee companies. Meanwhile, you can buy coffees such as Stewart's, Jewel 100% Colombian, and Eight O'Clock with a clear conscience.[83]

One of N2N's bulletins even stated that "P&G should boycott Salvadoran coffee, sending a clear signal to the Salvadoran oligarchy that they should support negotiations."[84] Among the actions used to threaten P & G were attempts to get grocery chains to comply with N2N's demands, on pain of picketing or other 'direct action.'[85] One attempt, detailed in an article titled "San Diego Chain Succumbs To ARENA Pressure," was to get the Big Bear Market chain in San Diego "reduce shelf space, post human rights warnings, stop advertising and cancel future purchases of Folger's!" Big Bear's failure to comply with these demands led to N2N's accusation that Big Bear was knuckling under to pressure from ARENA, and subsequently to what N2N describes as a 'media firestorm' (15 mentions in the local media) when N2N and the Central America Information Center (CAIC) picketed the chain's headquarters.[86]

One unusual tactic, of doubtful legality, was the 'stickering' of Folger's coffee cans in whatever store was under assault. Stickers offered for sale by the national organization featured a skull and crossbones with a choice of two messages: "Boycott Folger's!" or "Human rights warning!" followed by "This coffee helps fund Salvadoran death squads."[87] A local variation used by the Omaha branch appears to have been produced on a computer, and lacks the 'Jolly Roger.' A clearly illegal action, taken by several local groups, was the importation of Nicaraguan coffee in defiance of the embargo, presumably to replace the 'tainted' Salvadoran coffee with pure revolutionary brew.[88]

The boycott ran from November 1989 to January 1992, when N2N triumphantly announced its 'victory.'[89] In fact the campaign stalled with Folger's, and it appears that the boycott had very little effect beyond generating a certain amount of propaganda by the harassment of selected private companies, often by illegal means. If the boycott had actually succeeded staggering numbers of Salvadoran workers would have lost their jobs. Their spokesman's response to this possibility was that "in the long term they'll be better off."[90] Operating under the *cui bono* rule it seems obvious that the only real beneficiary of the coffee boycott would be the FMLN, which attempted to create and exploit economic turmoil to further its program of insurgency.

Most of the techniques above - even though they may involve deceptive propaganda - fall within the purview of freedom of speech. There were other means of support used, however, which cross the line into a gray area of legal interpretation; that of material support. In many cases they certainly violated the spirit of the Neutrality Act and other legislation, and in some cases clearly broke the law.

## Notes

1. Richard West, *Hurricane in Nicaragua* (New York: Viking Penguin, 1989), 58-59.

2. Ann Butwell, Washington Office on Latin America (WOLA), telephone interview with writer, 12 April 1991.
    WOLA is another Institute of Policy Studies spinoff.

3. Among the information distributed by CISPES to its affiliates was a detailed study of the foreign aid process titled *Understanding the Foreign Aid process in order to End War-related Aid to El Salvador* (undated), with 'pressure points' noted as being vulnerable to activist influence.

4. Ken Butigan, *The U.S. People Say NO: Nationwide Protest of U.S. Policy in El Salvador*, (Pledge of Resistance, 1989).

5. Angela Sanbrano, CISPES action/fundraising letter, circa 1989. This included an Action Message addressed to President Bush, to be signed and returned to CISPES.

6. Sanbrano, circa 1989.

7. These local affiliates can often be identified by the words "action," "response" or "mobilization" in their names.

8. Angela Sanbrano, CISPES action/fundraising letter, circa 1987.
This included a "Pledge for Peace" to be sent along with a financial contribution.

9. Castellanos, 28.

10. Van Gosse, 26.

11. Typical example: undated (circa January 1990) Pax Christi letter with "March 26: * Nonviolent civil disobedience action planned." Many such action bulletins featured "civil disobedience," sometimes using the phrasing "with the option for civil disobedience," as in a Pax Christi letter dated September 4, 1991.

12. Eric Pianin, "U.S. Behind Breakins, Sanctuary Leaders Testify," *The Washington Post*, February 20, 1987, A27.
The 'sanctuary' movement operated in open defiance of U.S. law and several members were jailed for their activities. As revealed in an undated (circa 1987) fundraising letter signed by Reverend Gustav H. Schultz for the National Sanctuary Defense Fund, the movement's position was that their superior morality placed them above the letter of the law.
House 100-42, 89-95.
However, according to Reverend Schultz's testimony during House hearings in February 1987 (on accusations that the FBI was breaking into 'sanctuary' churches), this law was to be strictly observed by others, especially any who opposed the 'sanctuary' movement.

13. Angela Sanbrano, action/fundraising letter, circa 1987. In her postscript Sanbrano suggests that "Your check for $100 or more may be tax-deductible if made payable to the 'CISPES Education Fund.'" This was to pay for CISPES' "educational work."

14. The FMLN was badly mauled in the field by such troops, and so quite naturally the FMLN support networks targeted the SOA for attack.

15. SOA Watch, The U.S. Army School of the Americas, undated (circa 1990).

16. Low intensity conflict is not even a "strategy." It is best defined as "the range of activities and operations on the lower end of the conflict spectrum involving the use of military or a variety of semi-military forces (both combat and noncombat) on the part of the intervening power to influence and compel the adversary to accept a political-military condition." Sam C.

Sarkesian and William L. Scully, eds., *US Policy and Low Intensity Conflict: Potentials for Military Struggles in the 1980s* (New York: National Defense Information Center, Inc., 1981), 2.

As quoted in David J. Dean, *The Air Force Role in Low-Intensity Conflict* (Maxwell AFB AL: Air University Press, 1986), 2.

Far from being victims of LIC, the FMLN and its supporters were actually *engaged* in low intensity conflict. The U.S. based support networks (including CISPES and SOA Watch) were part of the FMLN's 'low intensity war' as a "noncombat" force being used to "compel the adversary to accept a political-military condition."

17. Berryman, 44-45.
Senate 101-46, 67.
CISPES reprinted and distributed this forgery, and one dispute in the 1989 Senate hearings was whether or not CISPES knew it was a KGB product when it did so.

18. Berryman, 46-47.

19. United States Department of State, *Communist interference in El Salvador: documents demonstrating Communist support of the Salvadoran insurgency* (Washington DC: Government Printing Office, 1981).

This package provides copies of both the original documents and translations used to support the white paper. The three methods of delivery described - by boat, modified tractor-trailer, and airplane - were confirmed by numerous sources as being used (with variations) throughout the war. The types of weapons in the documents match those captured later on the battlefield and those described by other observers, such as Charles Clements.

20. Clements, 53-54.

21. Clements; 83, 134 & 236.

22. Castellanos, 36.
*Communist Interference in El Salvador*, 141-142.

23. Greg Walker, telephone interview 05 March 1993.

24. *Communist Interference in El Salvador,* 141-142.
"El Salvador's Army Displays Captured Arms," *The Washington Post*, 01 June 1989, A29.

Wilson Ring, "Honduras Says It Seized Arms Bound for Salvadoran Rebels," *The Washington Post*, 20 Oct 1989, A35.

25. Embassy of El Salvador press release, ca. September 1990.

26. Waller, 238.
This information was taken from a shipping document reproduced in Appendix 4 of Mr. Waller's book. This invoice was recovered from the glove box of the van. Oxfam was known to be sympathetic to both the Sandinistas and the FMLN.

27. Waller, 237.

28. Peter G. Kokalis, "The Combloc Connection," *Soldier of Fortune*, July 1990, 40.

29. Castellanos, 36.

30. Bill Gertz, "FMLN armed from Nicaraguan airstrip," *Washington* (D.C.) *Times*, 5 December 1989, NEWSBANK 1989 INT 135:F3.
Soviet- or Polish-built Antonov An-2's are better bushplanes, but their use by the Sandinistas would have been a dead giveaway.

31. William Branigan and Lee Hockstadter, "Airstrip Links Sandinistas to Arms Flights," *The Washington Post*, 04 December 1989, A1 & A31.

32. Lee Hockstadter and Douglas Farah, "Arms Cargo Found at Crash Site," *The Washington Post*, 26 November 1989, A1 & A30.

33. Dayna Smith and Douglas Farah, "Rebel Arms Carried Off By Ox Cart," *The Washington Post*, 28 November 1989, A19.

34. Castellanos, 38.

35. Edward C. Ezell, *Small Arms Today, 2nd Edition* (Harrisburg PA: Stackpole Books, 1988), 140.

36. "Shafik Handal's Travel Notes," reprinted in Ra'anan, Pfaltzgraff, et al, 335.

37. Ezell, 138-139.

38. Edward C. Ezell, *Small Arms Today*, (Harrisburg PA: Stackpole Books, 1984), 75.

39. *Communist Interference in El Salvador*, 3 & 75.

40. *Communist Interference in El Salvador*, 122.
Clements, 124.

41. "Guerrillas Use 'Plamya Shotgun'," *International Defense Review*, December 1988, 1559.

Peter G. Kokalis, "SOF T & Es New Combloc 30mm Launcher and Grenade," *Soldier of Fortune*, October 1991, 35.

Actually, the VOG-17 was a high velocity round with too high a recoil impulse to be employed safely in a shoulder fired weapon. According to Peter Kokalis, the round used was the externally similar but lower velocity - using a 'high-low' pressure propellant system similar to U.S. 40mm grenade rounds - VOG-26, which has never been encountered elsewhere. Kokalis speculated that the origin of the launcher was Cuba, and that the grenade was developed for them by the Soviets.

42. John M. Goshko, "Bush to Press Gorbachev on Central America," *The Washington Post*, 28 November 1989, A1 & A18.

43. "El Salvador's Army Displays Captured Items," *The Washington Post*, 01 June 1989, A29.

44. Wilson Ring, "Honduras says it Seized Arms Bound for Salvadoran Rebels," *The Washington Post*, 20 October 1989.

45. House 100-42, 114.

46. Peter LaBarbera, "Salvador rebels' allies leap into action here," *Washington* (D.C.) *Times*, November 24, 1989, NEWSBANK 1989 123:D4.

47. Angela Sanbrano, CISPES action/fundraising letter, circa 1989.

This gives 70,000 as the toll up to 1989, and may be considered reasonably official since she was CISPES Executive Director at the time. The figure of 75,000 appeared quickly thereafter in, among other places, an article by Cino Colina, "Martyrs of Christianity," *Granma* (English edition), 28 January 1990, 11.

48. U.S. Department of State, unclassified message titled *Salvadoran Deaths Due to War 1980-1991*, 26 March 1992.

49. Cynthia Arnson, Americas Watch, telephone interview 17 Feb 93.

50. *Salvadoran Deaths Due to War 1980-1991*, 26 March 1992.

51. Military dead according to these figures total 22,410 (U.S. Embassy) to 32,610 (Salvadoran Army).

52. *Salvadoran Deaths Due to War 1980-1991*, 26 March 1992.

53. Cynthia Arnson, 17 Feb 93.

54. *Statistical Abstract of Latin America*, Vol. 22, ed. James W. Wilkie & Stephen Haber, (Los Angeles: UCLA Latin American Center Publications, 1983), 112.
For comparison, this is in the same range as the Dallas rate of 36.0, and lower than Washington, D.C., at 59.5, and Detroit, with 57.9. All are 1988 figures from *The 1992 Information Please Almanac*, ed. Otto Johnson & Vera Dailey, (Boston: Houghton Mifflin, 1992), 829.

55. Americas Watch, *Violations of Fair trial Guarantees by the FMLN's ad hoc Courts*, May 1990, 18.
One specific case is of Norberto Velasco Rivas, described as a "former guerrilla" who was beaten and shot by men in Army uniforms "who called themselves 'the authorities'" on 11 January 1988. The FMLN took credit for the murder seven months later in a letter to Americas Watch dated 10 August 1988.

56. Douglas Farah, "Left Killed Activist, Says Duarte," *The Washington Post*, 6 January 1988, A15 & A19.

57. Castellanos, 49.

58. Clements, 156.

59. "Moderation Caught in a Cross Fire," (Washington D.C.) *Insight/Washington Times*, December 11, 1989, NEWSBANK 1989 INT 135:G5.

60. "The El Salvador Horror," *The New Republic*, December 11, 1989, 7.

61. Peter LaBarbera, "Salvador rebels' allies leap into action here," *Washington* (D.C.) *Times*, November 24, 1989, NEWSBANK 1989 123:D4.

62. In CISPES propaganda this was probably to show the FMLN combatants as 'being one with the people.' Much of such photography shows every indication of being posed.

63. Clements, photograph section between 144 & 145.

64. Schwartz, 41-42.
As Schwartz pointed out, this assertion is not necessarily false, but there is not sufficient hard evidence that it is true. Even the March 1993 UN Truth Commission report does not support this conclusion.

65. Schwartz, 41.

66. David Asman, "El Salvador's Guerrillas: Brutal Relics of the God That Failed," *The Wall Street Journal*, 8 March 1991, A11.

67. Central Intelligence Agency, *The World Factbook 1987* (Washington DC: Government Printing Office, 1987), 73.

68. Ivan Musicant, *The Banana Wars* (New York: MacMillan Publishing Company, 1990), 9.

69. Robert J. McCartney, "Salvadoran Rebel Unit Claims Killing of Marines, Not Others," *The Washington Post*, 22 June 1985, A1.
An FMLN communique taking credit for the Zona Rosa killings termed the massacre "execution of the political-military operation called: Yankee Aggressor in El Salvador, Another Vietnam Awaits You . . ."

70. *Statistical Abstract of Latin America*, Vol. 28, Table 2812, 824.

71. *Statistical Abstract of Latin America*, Vol. 28, Table 2806, 821.

72. Ambrose Evans-Pritchard, "Nicaragua's Killing Fields," *National Review*, 29 April 1991, 39.

73. Neighbor to Neighbor spokesperson, telephone interview by writer, 19 Apr 1991.

74. *Salvadoran Coffee Boycott Action Guide - Spring 1990* (San Francisco: Neighbor to Neighbor, 1990), 1.

> What do the Salvadoran people think? Neighbor to Neighbor talked to Salvadorans representing labor, church, and grassroots organizations. They support the boycott. Salvadoran endorsements included the largest labor federation, the National Union of Salvadoran Workers (UNTS), [and] the [Con]Federation of Associations of Cooperatives (COACES).

House 100-42, 30.
The UNTS was not the "largest labor federation." Despite a CISPES claim of 300,000 members, it actually had a total of 55,000 (not all of whom actually supported the FMLN - some groups later withdrew due to ideological differences) in 1986, while the independent National Workers--Campesino's Union (UNOC) had 215,000 to 250,000.

Radu & Tismaneanu, 191. The UNTS was controlled by several FMLN elements, particularly the PCES.

Castellanos, 77 & Appendix A. COACES was a rural FMLN/FDR "political/mass organization" under the DRU.

75. "El Salvador," *Country Profile*, U.S. Department of State, June 1990.

76. Captured FMLN Document, "Operational Modes We Will Use," *El Salvador at War*, ed. Max G. Manwaring and Court Prisk, with a preface by Edwin G. Corr (Washington DC: National Defense University Press, 1988), 358.

77. "Neighbor to Neighbor" spokesperson, telephone interview by writer, 19 Apr 1991.

78. "Want a really satisfying cup of coffee? DON'T DRINK FOLGER'S," Neighbor to Neighbor, circa 1990.

79. "The Attack on Salvadoran Coffee," *What's Happening*, Institute of Salvadoran Students and Alumni, July 1990.

80. "The Attack on Salvadoran Coffee," *What's Happening*, Institute of Salvadoran Students and Alumni, July 1990.

81. "Want a really satisfying cup of coffee? DON'T DRINK FOLGER'S," Neighbor to Neighbor, circa 1990.

82. Arthur Golden, "Talk of peace has Salvador coffee fields brewing anew," *San Diego* (California) *Union*, 8 October 1989, NEWSBANK 1989 INT 111:B4.

83. "Want a really satisfying cup of coffee? DON'T DRINK FOLGER'S," Neighbor to Neighbor, circa 1990.

84. Action Alert: "Urge Procter & Gamble To Take A Stand," *Grounds For Action*, May 1991, 3.

85. N2N *Action Guide*, Spring 1990, 3.

86. *Grounds For Action*, May 1991, 3.

87. N2N *Action Guide*, Spring 1990, 5.

88. *What Coffee Can I Drink?*, Neighbor to Neighbor, circa 1990.
"100% Nicaraguan coffee may be ordered from Pueblo to People at Ph: 1 (800) 843-5257." Having just recommended violating the law, the pamphlet goes on to state: "We want the coffee companies to realize NOW that it is not only morally right but wise business to cooperate with the boycott."
OCART, "Minutes from August 5, 1990 meeting," under "Other items discussed:" heading. "d.Obtaining Nicaraguan coffee from the Eastern Nebraska Socialist Party."

89. Alexis Gonzales and Carol Lynne D'Arcangelis, "N2N Lifts Boycott of Salvadoran Coffee - Launches Next Phase of Campaign," *Grounds For Action*, April-May 1992, 1.

90. N2N spokesperson, 19 Apr 1991.

## Chapter 7

# Private Intervention

One criticism of U.S. economic aid is that it only benefited a tiny proportion of the Salvadoran population.[1] The aid sent by the FMLN networks appears to have been even more narrowly focused. In every case where a destination was identified, it was in an FMLN-controlled zone or to an FMLN-associated organization. The bulk of it appears to have been intended to support the 'masas' - the hardcore guerrilla sympathizers - in areas where the FMLN had deliberately extirpated all of what government services there were.[2] The networks, especially MAES, SHARE, and the Sister City projects, provided the substitute services the FMLN/FDR needed in 8order to give itself some veneer of legitimacy as an alternate government. But not all of the aid went to 'civilians.' Much of it went, and was intended to go, to support FMLN combat operations in the field.

## Fundraising

In the early to middle 1980s the most important source of FMLN finance was the solidarity network in "Western Europe, the United States, Canada, and other Latin American countries."[3] According to captured records, in 1983 the PRTC received $389,954 - 94% of its revenues - from direct donations. Based on the PRTC being the smallest group, and assuming the other FMLN tendencies received similar amounts, it has been estimated that the FMLN took in $4 million in monetary donations during 1983.[4]

Fundraising activities took many forms, such as "Give-Peace-A--Dance" 'danceathons' in Berkeley, direct mail appeals from celebrities, dinners, and CISPES conventions.[5] There was even a book, *How To Make The World A Better Place*, which advocated contributions to CISPES as a concrete action to "make the world a better place."[6]

Of course, the fact that donations to CISPES and related organizations went to fund a program of assassination, sabotage, car bombs, and other such activities was denied, for very good reasons, most having to do with the wording of such legislation as the Foreign Agents Registration Act, the Neutrality Act, and the counterterrorism guidelines in the Foreign Intelligence Surveillance Act. All aid was characterized as 'humanitarian' and thus sanctified in the public view and rendered acceptable in the legal sense. There are four problems with this.

1. CISPES itself is on record as having opposed even humanitarian aid to the Nicaraguan Resistance, on the grounds that such aid helped the Contras' war effort. The authors of 'principled realism' urged a cutoff of all aid - including humanitarian - to distasteful regimes, on the same basis.

2. The FMLN itself saw 'non-military' aid as vital. According to captured PRTC financial documents its projected financial outlay for 1984 was $580,000, most of which was earmarked for "housing, food, and health-related expenditures."[7] One of the FMLN's greatest disappointments with the socialist bloc was the latter's generosity with weapons but penurious monetary assistance.[8] Priority items on Shafik Handal's 1980 'shopping trip' were uniforms, field first aid

kits, medical packs, medicines, radios, megaphones, batteries (for the radios and megaphones), boots, and money.[9]

3. Even if devoted exclusively to 'non-military' uses, all aid was clearly fungible; that is, it freed up resources to be employed for other, more overtly military, purposes.

4. No evidence has ever been made public that funds raised by the FMLN's support groups were strictly segregated by intended purpose once they were received. There is, on the other hand, considerable evidence that the opposite is true.

During House hearings on 19 and 20 February, 1987, CISPES spokesman Michael Lent waffled frantically when asked (on the basis of doubts raised by two *Washington Times* articles) what precisely was done with the donations being collected, until rescued by his lawyers, a Ms. and Mr. Ratner from the Center for Constitutional Rights (CCR).[10] The latter huffed that such questions were behind why FBI agents felt justified harassing such innocents as CISPES, and why wasn't the FBI investigating private aid to the Contras? (Which it was.)[11]

Lent never did answer the questions, and his lawyers clearly didn't want him to. If CISPES was so open, legal, and aboveboard, why did Lent and the Ratners evade this very pertinent question? The answer is that despite elaborate balance sheets drawn up by such organizations as CISPES and NEST, it appears that money and supplies were simply handed over to the FMLN and utilized as the latter saw fit. "The money raised by the US relief efforts is supposed to go to schools and hospitals and other projects in guerrilla held areas of El Salvador. But most of the donations end up financing the rebels."[12] The mechanism used was for the FMLN/FDR to set up and operate 'economic development' front organizations. An example would be the Social Action Investment Center (CIAS) which was organized by the FDR in 1981.[13]

> The CIAS collected donations from humanitarian organizations and the general public specifically to support FMLN projects in El Salvador. The projects were in areas of strong FMLN persistence and directed to their "masas" support base. A typical project involved the purchase of seed and fertilizer for peasant

followers of the FPL. According to Castellanos, many of the projects were fictitious, created to impress westerners with the FPL's technical sophistication, compassion, and economic need. Only about 30 percent of these donations actually reached the projects: the FPL used the other 70 percent to maintain its combatants.[14]

An even more egregious example was a project for a "student-run clinic and pharmacy at the National University." In August 1985 Medical Aid For El Salvador donated $195,000 worth of medical supplies to this project, which simply never happened.[15] As an aside, although Representative Pat Schroeder was briefed on this scam during hearings on 19 and 20 February 1987, she still endorsed a similar MAES project that September.[16] If all of this smacks somewhat of fraud, it has been called that before, apparently with no effect on the groups involved, and with all attempts at legal investigation being attacked as violations of CISPES' constitutional rights.[17]

In other countries the networks were more honest; for example, in West Germany a program called "Arms for El Salvador" netted the FPL $2 million in 1982.[18] Among its own members CISPES was somewhat more forthcoming about its actual intentions. In January, 1990, it held a convention to raise money for another "coming military offensive in San Salvador."

> The money, solicited Saturday at the third annual CISPES convention, would help enable Salvadoran guerrillas to launch a second major uprising by paying for the construction of two mobile emergency hospitals, organizers said. Mike Davis, executive director of the U.S.-El Salvador Institute for Democratic Development, said the group hoped to raise $10,000 for the so-called Bravo Fund during the three day convention. The money would pay for two $5,000 hospitals: one in San Salvador, the country's capital, and another on the outskirts of town, he said. "You can decide today: Do you want the FMLN to stay on the periphery or move into the heart of San Salvador?" Mr. Davis asked a crowd of about 500 at the Trinity College auditorium.[19]

It would appear from the quotation above that Mike Davis, at least, had few illusions about what CISPES' 'humanitarian' aid was meant to accomplish. More evidence is provided by an ad titled "JOIN The Good Fight For Democracy. FUND El Salvador's FMLN." This ad named the "Bravo Fund" as a project of the U.S.-El Salvador Institute for Democratic Development, with Angela Sanbrano, Executive Director of CISPES, listed on its Board of Directors. Even more blatant was a pamphlet put out by CISPES itself which had, as "What You Can Do" to "Support El Salvador's Fight for Freedom," "Make a donation through the El Salvador Freedom Drive to the non-military projects of the FMLN." Clearly, CISPES support was meant to help the FMLN's combat capability, and the labeling of such aid as 'humanitarian' or 'non-military' was so that donors could plausibly deny that they knew what it was really for.

Charles Clements unintentionally shows just how 'non-military' such aid to the FMLN was. When medical supplies arrived from the U.S., the wishes of the donors were never even mentioned as it was divided up for ostensibly 'civilian' or 'military' use. From his account it appears that internal FMLN politics actually determined the allocation of such resources.[20] The donors may have massaged their consciences (or had them massaged for them by CISPES, MAES, SHARE, or their Sister City project) with the idea that their donations were going to hapless refugees, but in reality no such distinction was made when the supplies reached the hands of the FMLN. Other aid programs had similar aims, and similar mechanisms of plausible deniability built in.

**War Industry**

> There are two fundamental industries, of which one is the manufacture of shoes and leather goods. [The other is an armory.] It is not possible for a troop to walk without shoes in wooded zones, hilly, with many rocks and thorns. It is very difficult to march without shoes in such conditions; only the natives, and not all of them, can do it. The rest must have shoes.[21]
> 
> -Che Guevara

In 1984 an organization called New El Salvador Today (NEST) put out a flyer calling for donations to build a shoe factory in a 'liberated zone' of El Salvador. To support a population stated to be 605 persons, this 'workshop' was to turn out an initial production run of *3180* pairs of shoes over a six month period.[22]

> Given the huge need, we want to establish a shoe workshop that would, in part, provide new shoes and repair used ones. Six companeros will be able to produce 100 pairs of shoes per month and repair 430 per month.[23]

Admittedly, Central America is tough on shoes, but 605 people are unlikely to need five new or reconditioned pairs apiece over a period of six months. Considering that this was supposed to be a local project, one can't help but conclude that NEST knew quite well that some of this footwear would have to be exported. There is a pretense of "follow-up and control" with the statement that "Our government junta will respond to the donor regarding the use of funds and the development of projects. . . ."[24] And although the FMLN is listed on the "Advisory Council" to this "Popular Junta,"[25] there are two gimmicks built in which gave NEST a way to deny that its aid was going to the guerrillas.

1. There was no real specification as to whom the shoes were intended to go. The inference was, of course, to the local farmers. Thus NEST could plead ignorance if the shoes went to combatants.

2. Although donor funds were to be loosely controlled, the excess product (and it looks like there would be plenty) would be completely the property of the local 'junta.' Thus the funds from NEST could be laundered by selling the shoes, and the resulting revenues used for whatever purpose the 'junta' decided.

And even if NEST was sincerely concerned about where their donations were going, their only control mechanism was to ask the junta, which would "respond." So what was to keep the junta from simply lying? It is hard to imagine that people who were willing to murder one another over points of revolutionary theory would have much trouble telling sympathizers whatever they wanted to hear.

**The Repopulation Program**

> However active the leading group may be, its activity will amount to fruitless effort by a handful of people unless combined with the activity of the masses. On the other hand, if the masses alone are active without a strong leading group to organize their activity properly, such activity cannot be sustained
>
> for long, or carried forward in the right direction, or raised to a high level.[26]
>
> —Mao Tsetung

Guerrilla groups need a civilian population to hide behind and parasitize. One of the most serious problems facing the FMLN/FDR in the early 1980s was the loss of this population from their operating areas. Why people left is no mystery - wherever the FMLN existed in any force became a battlefield. The motivating factors behind the rural-urban migration pattern assumed a new dimension, and the FMLN's subject population was depleted. This dealt a crippling blow to the FMLN's logistics, communications and intelligence capabilities, and had serious effects on morale.[27]

All that were left were the "most radicalized" of the FMLN's hard-core supporters, called *masas* - literally, 'masses.' These 'masses' were not actually all that numerous, and apparently took their name from Marxist, especially Maoist, literature. Their small number was a problem; they provided a very shallow sea in which the guerrillas could swim. The FMLN's answer to this was repopulation of these 'liberated zones' with less committed *masas* and even ordinary refugees in the hope that they, too, could be radicalized.[28]

Thus were born such programs as Salvadoran Humanitarian Aid, Research, and Education Foundation's (SHARE) 'Going Home' campaign, in which, with criminal disregard for their welfare and safety, refugees were moved into war zones. Evidence of direct FMLN involvement with this campaign is provided by 'Going Home' literature which lists the Christian Committee for the Displaced of El Salvador (CRIPDES) as the Salvadoran organization with which the program was coordinated.[29] CRIPDES was established by the FMLN/FDR when CIAS was revealed as a scam being used to siphon humanitarian funds to the guerrilla's war effort, and appears to originally have had much the same purpose.[30]

CRIPDES obviously did not have the refugees' interests as its highest priority when it pushed to have civilians moved into 'liberated zones.' These areas were, as several observers have remarked, the worst possible places for the refugees to go.[31] Not surprisingly, though, the program was described in glowing terms by the FMLN support networks. A letter from Quest For Peace endorsing 'Going Home/SHARE' is fairly typical.

> The people of El Salvador are going home to the land they love, the earth which so many of their sisters and brothers have watered with their blood. They are returning to their communities from which they were driven by death squads, government army sweeps and aerial bombings. . . .
> . . . They do so because Salvadorans are passionate about their land and determined to have their "right to live and work in peace" respected.
> With your financial and political support, these people can realize their dream of returning home. . . .
> The next few months are critical for the repopulated communities. Join in, support SHARE's work with the repopulated villagers and tilt the outcome toward peace - and please be generous with your contributions and prayers.[32]

In reality the refugees were transplanted to areas laid waste by military action, which the FMLN had deliberately attempted to sever from government control - and thus what social services there had been - by programs of intimidation and assassination. Many refugees had originally fled from these communities precisely because their "right to live and work in peace" had been violated by the guerrillas.

> The guerrillas . . . tried to obligate these people to collaborate economically with them, to force people to give them money or food, and when people didn't have it or couldn't give it, to make people work for them. if they didn't do it, they were given some sanction and were accused of being reactionaries. This situation was very demoralizing because the people left.[33]

The repopulated zones had a shadow government organized by the FMLN/FDR. These FMLN-controlled, illegal 'local popular governments' (PPL) were the actual entities with which all the Sister City projects in El Salvador were established.[34] Since the FMLN could provide little in the way of material services, these became the responsibility of the support networks. For example, the programs supported by the Madison - Arcatao Sister City project included "Agricultural Production," "Education," "Health Care," and other "Community projects;" the last including "a community child care center, a store (all sales at cost), a bakery, and a chicken farm."[35]

Even with this effort, the population of *masas* was never very large, and certainly nowhere near a majority of the Salvadoran people. After the war, and thus after several years of the repopulation program, only 23,810 pro-FMLN 'repatriados' were living in 'liberated zones.'[36]

### 'Internationalist' Mercenaries

Leftist intervention was not limited to activities in the United States. Carroll Ishee was killed in August 1983 fighting alongside the FMLN in the Morazan province.[37] An account by his wife (taken from a CISPES document) is revealing:

> It was in LSM [the Liberation Student Movement] that I met my husband Carroll Ishee. In 1980, we moved to New Orleans as students with the intention of eventually travelling to Angola as brigadistas. The war in El Salvador changed that plan.
> After a difficult and painful winter of decision-making, we left school. In 1981 Carrol [sic] went to El Salvador as a militant and I became increasingly active in CISPES. In August 1983 Carroll was killed by U.S. helicopter fire as a member of the FMLN.[38]

Rebecca Tarver, an assistant editor of the CISPES newspaper *Alert!*, was wounded in combat and captured by the Salvadoran Army on 24 June 1990. She was marching with an FPL column, armed with an M-16, and had adopted the war-name 'Clara.' As a member of the FPL she held the rank of 'militant,' and was working with SALPRESS, the FMLN propaganda organization.[39] There are reports that other Americans were recruited into the FMLN - often members (especially officers) of support network organizations - and served in combat.[40] This is quite likely. CISPES and MAES (among other organizations) openly sent volunteers called 'brigadistas' to work - often in combat support roles - in rebel held areas.[41] To give some notion of the scale of this effort, "in January, 1983, it [MAES] spent 80,000 dollars to train and equip 110 medical 'brigadistas'."[42] Dr. Charles Clements, later involved with MAES, appears to have been an example of a medical 'brigadista' (probably better qualified than most) although he never applied the term to himself in his book. Passing himself off as a 'neutral non-combatant,' Dr. Clements operated only in an FMLN-controlled zone, often treated combatants, and even accompanied a guerrilla column during an attack.[43]

As an aside, Sandinista propaganda and "Miami Vice" notwithstanding, it thus appears that there were more documented American 'soldiers of fortune' serving with the FMLN than with the Nicaraguan Resistance. The northern - and larger - force in Nicaragua (the FDN) never accepted American volunteers. One American fought briefly in the southern force (ARDE), under Eden Pastora; Steve McAllister, also known as 'Peregrino,' who got into it virtually by accident (compounded by a certain amount of bad judgement). He was a 'war tourist' who went on patrol with a contra unit and ended up having to help them fight their way back out.[44]

As mentioned earlier, a church worker named Jennifer Jean Casolo was caught during the 1989 offensive with an arms cache in her back yard. According to one account it consisted of "103 grenades, 213 blocks of dynamite, 405 mine detonators, 150 feet of slow burning fuse, and hundreds of rounds for Soviet-made AK-47, Dragunov, and G-3 automatic rifles."[45] The indignation that followed her arrest is an emotional response stemming at least partly from her connection with 'the Church.' The fact is that radical Christians made up a substantial part of the FMLN, and such people as Ms. Casolo consistently abused their positions to help them.

> Salvadoran Attorney General Mauricio Eduardo Colorado says the government is striking against "terrorists" wherever it finds them. "The church itself is healthy," he told The Miami Herald in an interview, "but there are bad sons who abuse its shelter."[46]

Ms. Casolo was released, despite material and circumstantial evidence that she was guilty. Her partisans crowed that this meant the

Salvadoran government had no case against her.[47] In fact it did.[48] She was released solely because of political pressure, not on the basis of the evidence.[49] There are some irregularities which could be explained by a 'setup,' but assuming she is not simply lying, the most likely candidate for such an action is her friends in the FMLN. Certainly the propaganda generated benefited them more than anyone, and gave their network in the U.S. a *cause celebre*. She may be lucky that they did not feel the need for another martyr just then.

These are some of the means 'legal and illegal' employed by the FMLN's support network to help prosecute the Salvadoran civil war. When asked what motivated the members of this network to side with the FMLN, many answered with stories of right-wing atrocities, especially the murder of Archbishop Romero on March 24, 1980, and the Four Nuns (actually three nuns and a lay worker) on December 4th of the same year. Later, the murder of the Six Jesuits became the atrocity-of-choice.

**The Six Jesuits**

On November 16, 1989, six Jesuits, their housekeeper, and her daughter were murdered at the University of Central America in El Salvador.[50] Besides the simple barbarity of the killings, the act was a serious mistake. One of the objectives of the November 1989 guerrilla offensive was to provoke just such an overreaction. According to Miguel Castellanos, a former FMLN commandante, "They will try to provoke the security forces to take actions that will result in a cutoff of [U.S.] military aid."[51] The FMLN's allies were poised to exploit the resulting propaganda, and used the event to stake their claim to a moral high ground from which to denounce U.S. policy. But in light of their support for the FMLN was this claim to moral superiority justified?

**Notes**

1. Tom Barry and Deb Preusch, *The Soft War*, (New York: Grove Press, 1988), 257.
Barry and Preusch actually stated that U.S. foreign aid should be decoupled from considerations of national interest. They apparently view foreign aid as a sort of global welfare with the U.S. taxpayer footing the bill.

2. "The El Salvador Horror," *The New Republic*, 11 December 1989, 8.
Candidates of the Democratic Convergence (CD), a leftist party loosely allied with the FMLN, estimated FMLN adherents at 50,000.
Reliable figures of FMLN support in El Salvador or in the U.S. are impossible to get, according to Stanford professor Dr. Terry Karl (telephone interview 17 April 1991).
Embassy of El Salvador letter dated 23 April 1993.
A postwar ONUSAL survey put the total of FMLN adherents as 38,810 - 23,810 "repatriados" and 15,000 union members - plus 182,921 less-committed but largely sympathetic "desplazados" in refugee camps.

3. Unclassified State Department cable, reproduced in House 100-42, 18.

4. House 100-42, 18-19.

5. "Counterscandal: Private Gifts Load Guns for Marxist Rebels," (Washington D.C.) *Insight/Washington Times*, 9 February 1987, NEWSBANK 1987 INT 16:B10-11.

6. Jeffrey Hollender, *How to Make the World a Better Place - A Guide to Doing Good* (New York: William Morrow, 1989), Action 120.

7. House 100-42, 17.

8. House 100-42, 17.

9. *Communist Interference in El Salvador*, 45-47.

10. The essence of Lent's argument seems to have been along the lines of "if you don't already know about it, then it must not have happened."

11. House Subcommittee on Civil and Constitutional Rights, *Break-ins at Sanctuary Churches and Organizations Opposed to Administration Policy in Central America*, 100-42, (Washington DC: Government Printing Office, 1988), 169.

Geoffrey Morris, "Much Ado About Nothing," *National Review*, 29 April 1988, 42.
In fact the FBI did investigate private Contra support. The U.S. Council for World Freedom and the National Defense Council both opened their files and cooperated fully with the FBI investigations.
Not only did CISPES refuse to open its files or in any other way cooperate, but it sued to get everything the FBI might already have on CISPES.

12. "Counterscandal: Private Gifts Load Guns for Marxist Rebels," B11.

13. House 100-42, 19.

14. House 100-42, 19-20.

15. House 100-42, 36.

16. Patricia Schroeder, endorsement letter for MAES, dated 16 September 1987.

17. James Morrison, "Salvadoran rebels bilk donors in U.S.", *Washington (D.C.) Times*, 23 January 1987, NEWSBANK 1987 INT 16:B6.

18. House 100-42, 18.

19. Valerie Richardson, "Salvador rebels promise blood, get cash," *Washington (D.C.) Times*, 15 January 1990, NEWSBANK 1990 INT 2:B12.

20. Clements, 147-150.
Clements does mention one case where money given to him specifically for pediatric care was used to buy powdered milk; 96.

21. Guevara, 142.

22. Some of these observations also appear in an article by Michael Boos, "Group in Nation's Capital to Aid Left-wing Terrorists," dated 25 June 1984 and proposed for *The American Sentinel*. This article was reproduced in House Subcommittee on Civil and Constitutional Rights, *CISPES and FBI Counterterrorism Investigations*, 100-122, (Washington DC: Government Printing Office, 1989), 379-382.

23. New El Salvador Today (NEST) pamphlet, *Project for Agriculture, Health and a Shoe Factory for the Local Popular Government of Tequeque, Los Albertos and Los Dubon, Chalatenango Province*, undated.
Reproduced in House 100-122, 389.
Gus Newport was on the Board of Directors of NEST, and was also mayor of Berkeley at the time. These communities are stated as being part of the municipality of Arcatao, which has been a Sister City of Madison, Wisconsin since April 1, 1986. These 'local popular governments' were not the legal governments of these communities, and the 'Sister City' connection had nothing to do with Sister Cities International.

24. House 100-122, 390.

25. House 100-122, 391.

26. Mao Tsetung, 131-132.

27. Castellanos, 93.

28. Castellanos, 93.

29. Newton (KS) Area Peace Center, letter dated 25 June 1990.

30. House 100-42, 21.

31. Tammy Arbuckle, "El Salvador: the real war in Central America?" *International Defense Review*, February 1989, 159.

32. William R. Callahan, sj, and Dolores C. Pomerleau, "An Urgent Plea," Quest for Peace endorsement letter for SHARE's "Interfaith Campaign in Support of Salvadoran Refugees Returning From Exile in Mesa Grande" (Honduras), undated.

33. Castellanos, 93.

34. NEST pamphlet reproduced in House 100-122, 391.
This page shows a diagram of the "Local Popular Government Structure," with the FMLN on the "Advisory Council." The pamphlet's cover (p. 383) lists Sandra Serpas as "Sister Cities Coordinator." This was not Sister Cities International (SCI), but the National Center for U.S.-El Salvador Sister Cities, which has no connection with SCI.

## Private Intervention 123

35. *Madison Arcatao Sister City Project: Rebuilding our Sister City*, undated. This describes the repopulation effort in the usual glowing terms, and gives April 1, 1986 as the establishment date for this program. Robert Kastenmeier (D-WI) is listed on the "Board of Endorsers." Arcatao was also the focus of the NEST program mentioned earlier. It must be emphasized that it was not the legal, elected government of Arcatao, but an FMLN front organization with which Madison allied itself.

36. ONUSAL survey, quoted in letter from the Embassy of El Salvador, 23 April 1993.

37. Jeff Jones, ed., *Brigadista: Harvest and War in Nicaragua* (New York: Praeger Publishers, 1986), Dedication.

38. LaVaun Ishee, CISPES Southeast Regional Coordinator, in biography distributed at CISPES 1985 National Convention.
As quoted by Waller, 224.

39. Waller, 157-158.

40. "El Salvador: Two Americans Murdered," *For Your Eyes Only*, January 1991, 257-7.
Radu & Tismaneanu, 203.
This also lists Dutch, Italian, Spanish, and Nicaraguan volunteers as among the foreigners serving with the FPL. "Most of these foreigners are medical and political support personnel, but some are counterintelligence and weapons specialists."

41. CISPES spokesperson, telephone interview by writer, 22 May 1991.
House 100-42, 36.

42. House 100-42, 36.
A MAES fundraising letter dated 12 December 1989, refers to its "121 'barefoot' doctors" (highly doubtful in a literal sense) as one of its "unique" ongoing programs.

43. Clements; 15 (neutrality), 6 (serving in guerrilla held area), 51 (treating combatants), 81-90 (marching with guerrilla column).
A closer approximation of his actual role would be as a combat medic engaged in a civic action project; in this case for the FMLN.

44. Marty Casey, telephone interview by writer, 10 May 1991.

45. Christopher Marquis, "Salvador arrest hints a new policy," *Miami* (Florida) *Herald*, 3 December 1989, NEWSBANK 1989 INT 135:E3.

46. Marquis, 135:E2.

47. Mark Pazniokas and Erin Martin, "Casolo freed, expected back in state today," *Hartford* (Connecticut) *Courant*, 14 December 1989, NEWSBANK 1989 INT 135: B6-8.

48. Marquis, 135:E3.

49. "A Church Worker in Central America," *People's Daily World*, 5 January 1990.
As quoted in "Casolo & CISPES", *Soldier of Fortune*, May 1990, 33.
"She was released only after intense international pressure."

50. Jose Z. Garcia, "Tragedy in El Salvador," *Current History*, January 1990, 12.

51. Morton M. Kondracke, "Salvador's Silver Lining," *The New Republic*, 13 March 1989, 23.
Castellanos said this during an interview with Mr. Kondracke on 15 Feb 89. The next day he was assassinated by the FMLN. His real name was Napoleon Romero Garcia and his case is covered briefly in the May 1990 Americas Watch study.

**Chapter 8**

# The FMLN: Terrorists or Guerrillas?

That the FMLN committed acts of terrorism is undeniable. Thus the question becomes, rather, was the FMLN a terrorist organization or was it a guerrilla organization which used terrorism as a tactic?

> The United States has sought to portray the FMLN as a terrorist movement. But the FMLN does not have roots in religious or nationalist protest that would force it to turn to fanaticism. The FMLN is not a terrorist organization. Its military practices seek to win the support of society, not to intentionally and premeditatively cause civilian casualties.[1]
> 
> -Joaquin Villalobos

In 1987 Tutela Legal, the Catholic Church human rights monitoring organization, attributed more political murders to the FMLN than to rightist death squads.[2] That same year the U.S. Embassy "laid seven political killings to the military and extreme right, 205 to the FMLN, and 14 to unknown assailants, with 184 other "suspicious murders."[3]

## Assassination and the 'War of the Mayors'

A serious embarrassment to the Sandinistas (especially considering their officially neutral status in the Salvadoran civil war) was the brutal murder of a ranking member of the FMLN in Managua - Dr. Melida Anaya Montes - on 6 April 1983, because of one of the FMLN's continuing ideological disputes. Cayetano Carpio ('Commandante General Marcial') committed suicide over this incident (on the advice of Tomas Borge, and in lieu of an embarrassing trial).[4] Such events were by no means rare - the FMLN has a history of 'pruning' its own cadres. One of the more interesting characters encountered by Charles Clements was 'Pedro,' an FMLN assassin whose entire mission was to travel around eliminating 'traitors.'[5]

The FMLN did not limit assassination to ideological dissenters within its own ranks. Its campaign against rural mayors can be illustrated by the experience of the town of San Jorge. On May 3, 1985, three FMLN guerrillas took the newly elected mayor, Mauricio Valenzuela, to a small church and shot him, possibly after some parody of a trial. He was the third to be murdered since the beginning of the war. "There was no motive for the killing. He was a well liked man who tried not to take sides in the conflict," his sister was quoted as saying. His eight year old niece said: "He was a good man but they took him and killed him. Now I am scared."[6]

This campaign quickened during 1988-1989, when what were described as 'dozens' of mayors resigned after being threatened by the FMLN. These were not empty threats.

> The threats have come after the Marxist-led Farabundo Marti National Liberation Front (FMLN) executed nine mayors in October and November as part of an effort to prove that the U.S. backed government, while able to carry out elections, cannot protect the civilian authorities.[7]

This attack on elected officials was not an isolated campaign. It was part of a much broader attempt by the FMLN to undermine the legitimacy of the government by completely destroying the democratic process in El Salvador. That this strategy involved terrorizing much of the populace and the targeted killing of individuals does not seem to have particularly disturbed either the FMLN or its 'human rights activist' supporters.

**Death Squads for Democracy**

Despite 'democratic' rhetoric,[8] the FMLN consistently attempted to disrupt every election from 1981 to 1991.[9] According to Charles Clements, the FMLN justified this by claiming that the elections were a fraud, and that they were giving the people an excuse not to participate. The government required everyone to vote, stamped their papers after they did, and used unstamped papers as a means of identifying possible guerrillas. By boycotting elections and shooting at voters the FMLN was actually doing those voters a favor.[10]

Figure 8. *Buses were a favorite FMLN target.*

The government stopped requiring people to vote, but the FMLN didn't stop disrupting elections. The result was lower voter turnout.[11] But those voters who did vote were obviously becoming fed up with the FMLN. Something of a watershed was reached in 1989. In the 1989 elections the FMLN "threatened with death anyone who voted, and sought to bring transportation to a standstill by mining roads and machine-gunning trucks, cars, and buses."[12]

> The rebels made an imposing display of violence. They assassinated eight rural mayors. They killed five civilians with car bombs placed near military sites in San Salvador. Urban commandos assassinated five prominent rightists, and are widely blamed for the murder of another. They knocked out the capital's water and electricity supply during election week and hit army positions in 20 towns on election day. All told, the Catholic Church says, the guerrillas were responsible for 26 targeted killings of civilians the first half of this year, and killed another 24 people with explosives.[13]

The ARENA party, already powerful in the judicial branch, managed to capture the legislative and executive branches of the Salvadoran government as well, elected by the lowest percentage of registered voters in the 1980's.[14] The FMLN support networks claimed that the elections were "a fraud" because the political parties participating "represent only some sectors of Salvadoran society" and because of the low voter turnout.[15] This was a very neat argument, since the FMLN/FDR deliberately refused to participate, and its terror campaign was apparently successful in frightening away many people who might otherwise have voted. This unequal representation (if it was unequal) was thus the FMLN's fault, and the FMLN must accept responsibility for putting ARENA into power.

Why this dichotomy between rhetoric and practice? Part of it was almost certainly for propaganda purposes; 'democracy' played better when courting international support, especially in the United States. Part of it was a matter of interpretation; the FMLN saw Castro's Cuba as a 'people's democracy,' which it would probably like to emulate.[16] But it appears that the actual basis for the FMLN's actions was that "evidence suggests that the FMLN's true popular support is in fact very limited, and that this is precisely why it has resorted to warfare, provocation, and terrorism."[17] In 1989 the Democratic Convergence (CD), a leftist party loosely connected with the FMLN through the FDR, estimated the FMLN's adherents as only 50,000.[18] A postwar United Nations survey turned up 38,810, plus 182,921 less-committed but largely sympathetic "desplazados."[19] Even adding these last two numbers together gives only 221,731, which is less than half of the 510,126 who voted for ARENA in the 19 March 1989 elections.[20]

## The Zona Rosa Massacre

A survey of the FMLN's death squad activities is available in an Americas Watch study titled *Violation of Fair Trial Guarantees by the FMLN's Ad Hoc Courts* (May 1990). The reason for the cumbersome title is that the FMLN often took the legalistic step of declaring a victim to have been tried and condemned to death by one of their 'ad hoc' (kangaroo) courts. But "[g]overnment officials are not the only victims of the rebels' summary justice.'" They've also murdered "coffee farm workers, people who defy transport strikes, members who quit the movement and peasants who resist paying 'war taxes.'"[21] One case not covered by the Americas Watch study was the murder of six Americans, five Salvadorans, a Guatemalan, and a Chilean at a sidewalk cafe in the Zona Rosa section of El Salvador on June 19, 1985.[22]

> The gunmen were dressed as regular army soldiers. "A Datsun pickup truck with anywhere from six to 10 men in camouflage uniforms pulled up beside a cafe in one of San Salvador's nightclub districts," said Chief U.S. Embassy spokesman Donald Hamilton. "These terrorists opened fire with automatic weapons across what amounted to nearly a block of wall-to-wall cafes." Bodies of the dead and wounded lying in pools of their own blood were strewn across the floors of the restaurants.[23]

Four of the Americans were Marine guards from the Embassy. Two were businessmen, specifically Wang computer salesmen. None were armed, nor were any involved in military operations against the FMLN, which claimed credit for the attack with the following radio announcement.

> On Wednesday, 19 June, six U.S. advisers [sic] were justly punished. They were annihilated at a restaurant in the San Benito neighborhood by FMLN guerrilla commandos. . . . The FMLN's actions against the Yankee invaders will be expanded, both in number and nature. . . . The execution of these military men

> [sic, for the computer salesmen] is an act of revolutionary justice.[24]

The other seven victims were bystanders. The investigation into this attack is incomplete. Three of the triggermen were convicted and sentenced to "prison terms ranging from four to 25 years" on 3 May 1991.[25] However, although many of the members of the network responsible were arrested, most were released in exchange for President Duarte's daughter, Ines Guadalupe Duarte Duran, who was kidnapped by the FMLN.[26]

Predictably, the CISPES reaction to the killings was to make excuses for the FMLN.[27] The FMLN characterization of the victims as 'advisers' has been widely accepted in the support networks. A Pax Christi spokesperson seemed to consider the presence of the Marines in El Salvador to be proof that they were advisers, because if they weren't, "then what were they doing there?"[28] Actually, in accordance with Foreign Affairs Manual 12 FAM 340, Marines are stationed at all United States embassies as guards. They are not 'advisers' or 'trainers,' and thus can only be considered combatants by organizations at war with the United States as a whole. This action conclusively proved that the FMLN was indeed at war with the United States in every way short of reciprocal declaration. It was also the largest single massacre of Americans by the FMLN, which killed at least eight others, five of whom were military.[29]

**Fundraising**

Besides their solidarity organizations, the FMLN/FDR had alternative sources of funds. According to Frank McNeil, the FMLN started the war with a fairly sizeable "war chest," which it obtained primarily through kidnapping, its favorite 'fundraising' technique during the 1970s.

> The insurgent factions had amassed from kidnappings a war chest of perhaps $30 million . . . Price Waterhouse does not audit insurgents' books, but all that probably didn't go to revolutionary purposes. In every movement, there are cadres

who believe Lenin intended for them to live well, just as some evangelists believe God wills a gaudy lifestyle.[30]

Many of the victims were murdered after the ransom was safely paid. One, Ambassador Beneke, was apparently declared an enemy of the people for "open[ing] up the Japanese market to Salvadoran coffee."[31] This remained a favored domestic source of revenue throughout the war, but after 1985 it became more important due to the drop in 'solidarity' donations.[32]

> The FMLN does not discriminate in the selection of its victims; it kidnaps small cotton farmers in Usulutan and big businessmen in San Salvador. A survey of recent incidents shows that ransoms range from as little as $20 to more than $60,000, with the bulk in the $4,000 to $5,000 range. . . .
> Although potentially far more lucrative than contributions from collaborators, this strategy is problematic. It is difficult and expensive to create urban commando units which are capable of carrying out successful kidnappings. The task is all the more difficult now, because the urban infrastructure of the guerrillas is in a shambles as a result of the government's thorough investigations of the Inez Duarte kidnapping and the Zona Rosa massacre. . . .
> As a result, FMLN groups have direct[ed] the bulk of their operations against small farmers in rural - and generally impoverished - areas. This places the self-proclaimed "Representatives of the People" in the uncomfortable position of victimizer. The victims rarely have anything to do with the government and are often individuals of modest means.[33]

'War taxes' were another source of revenue. 'War taxes' is a euphemism for robbery, murder and extortion, and in practice took two basic forms. In one, roadblocks were set up, and the occupants of stopped vehicles were 'taxed' of cash, watches, and other valuables at gunpoint. Inevitably, there were individuals who preferred not to stop for various reasons (usually self-preservation) and the guerrillas opened fire.[34] Since a high proportion of these vehicles were buses, many civilian casualties were attributed to this method.[35]

The other method was straightforward extortion. 'Taxpayers' were ordered to provide funds and supplies, or else.

> The manager of a small coffee farm received a form letter in late 1985 from the FMLN informing him that if he wished to harvest his coffee in peace, he had to:
> (A) Comply with the salary schedule endorsed by the FMLN;
> (B) Pay 10,000 colones in cash ($2,000);
> (C) Deliver 15 pounds of aluminum oxide, 10 pounds of potassium chlorate, 15 meters of slow wick, and 10 flares.
>
> The manager was given 17 days to purchase and deliver the cash and the goods.[36]

Another grower received a demand for "250,000 colones ($50,000), 100 pounds each of aluminum oxide and potassium chlorate, 200 blasting caps, and a rotary multicopier." Besides money, the FMLN often demanded "boots, materials for uniforms, and knapsacks."[37] As an additional benefit, such 'war taxes' appear to have served as part of the FMLN's campaign against the coffee industry, the U.S. portion of which was Neighbor to Neighbor's 'coffee boycott.'

**Economic Disruption**

The coffee industry was just one of the targets of the economic disruption campaign. Details of this guerrilla strategy came to light with the capture of a document titled "Operational Modes We Will Use." In it the FMLN stated that "sabotage and destabilization" of the economy and infrastructure was a "fundamental element" of its "strategic plan." A specific goal was to counteract U.S. assistance by preventing economic recovery, so that "many millions of dollars will be lost."[38] Economic targets listed in this document were:

a. Fuel
b. Electricity
c. Railroads
d. Telephonic communications (line and microwave)
e. Cotton and Coffee.[39]

Indeed, $2.1 billion of U.S. aid, which could have helped develop the general economy and benefit the majority of Salvadorans, was wasted repairing the damage of a guerrilla war funded (at least in part) by the U.S. FMLN support networks.[40] For example, during one attack on the Cerron Grande dam (a favorite target since it provided power for San Salvador) on 3 May 1991, a transformer worth $500,000 dollars was destroyed by one rocket propelled grenade. To keep the Salvadoran power grid operating in the face of such FMLN attacks cost the Agency for International Development (AID) $100 million for this program alone. Salvadoran linemen became expert at replacing destroyed towers, and even developed their own method for predicting when the FMLN would strike.[41]

> "We always know that when the guerrillas say we're going to have a truce, that's a sure tip-off that 15 days in advance there'll be a new surge of attacks on towers. And then of course during sugar and coffee harvests, during peace talks and election campaigns."[42]

To help the linemen keep up with their job's unusual demands, AID provided the electric company with two civilian helicopters. Besides the ordinary hazards electrical workers have to face, the FMLN did not always content itself with just blowing up facilities and equipment.

> The helicopters, which are unarmed, have been shot at. The rebels often leave land mines or booby traps around the toppled towers. Two linemen have been killed on the job and at least a dozen injured, three seriously enough to require amputation.[43]

## Mine Warfare

One the FMLN's favorite tactics was the large scale use of mines. This has been attributed to Vietnamese influence, but such mine warfare was popular with most leftist insurgencies as an economical method of causing casualties, and Guevara recommended it highly.[44] It does appear that the Vietnamese were closely involved with the actual mining operations, as evidenced by FMLN manuals on the subject having been "originally prepared in Hanoi."[45] According to Victor Rosello, mine use increased after 1984.

In the 1987-1988 midyear reporting period alone, the Salvadoran armed forces suffered a total of 2,019 casualties, of which 465 resulted in deaths. . . . Consistently between 45-80 percent of these casualties result from mines. Civilians are also victims of indiscriminate minings. Primarily homemade in fabrication, mines come in various shapes and sizes and may be either pressure or command detonated.[46]

The most common mines were "18cm-high PVC tubes filled with explosives and designed to maim rather than kill," because "wounded soldiers put a greater strain on Government logistics than dead ones."[47] Of course, such plastic mines were undetectable by ordinary mine detectors (which are actually metal detectors), and their use was effective as a denial tactic since Army patrols were often reluctant to operate in areas where mines were thought to be emplaced.[48]

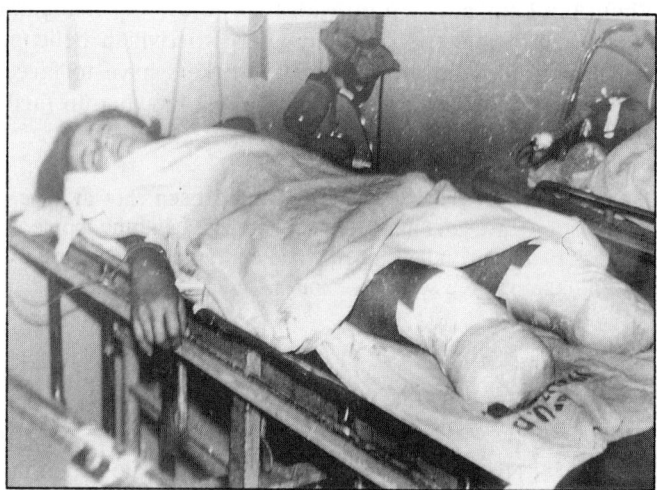

**Figure 9.** *Soldiers were not the only victims of FMLN mines.*

Mines are, by their very nature, not a discriminating weapon, and in El Salvador soldiers were not their only victims. Civilian trucks, buses and private automobiles were frequently damaged or destroyed when the FMLN mined roads during their periodic transportation stoppages.[49] The FMLN's theory seems to have been that anyone still attempting to travel was a de facto government collaborator and therefore a legitimate target. Anti-personnel mines killed and maimed still more civilians. In *Witness to War* Clements related such an incident where a *campesino* ran afoul of an FMLN boobytrap and was mortally wounded.[50]

**Terrorists or Freedom Fighters?**

So was the FMLN a terrorist organization? It clearly engaged in deliberate political murder, used tactics that caused civilian casualties, and organized violent crime as a basic domestic source of financial support. To its victims the difference between criminal terrorists and such a guerrilla group using terrorism is effectively nil. To attempt to excuse such actions because of the supposedly high motives of the perpetrators is hypocritical, especially if similar atrocities committed by their opposition - who may simply have different ideals - are to be condemned on an objective basis. Idealism and fervor are not reliable touchstones for the truth. Hitler and his National Socialist Workers Party were both idealistic and fervent. That their ideals were warped and their energy misdirected seems obvious now, but at the time millions were swept up in the Nazi crusade.

Terrorists or not, what is clear is that the FMLN saw itself as being at war with the United States, and justified its actions on that basis. That this status was not officially recognized by the United States at the time (apparently due to political sensitivities based on the "'no more Vietnams' hysteria")[51] does not diminish the fact, much as the similar lack of formal declaration did not make U.S. involvement in the Southeast Asian conflict any less a war.

This brings up an interesting legal and moral question. Since the FMLN was at war with the United States, did that make any knowing American supporter of the FMLN a traitor in wartime? By playing with semantics and legalism, FMLN supporters may be able protect their activities as 'dissent.' But it seems clear that in a moral and practical sense their activities were nothing less than treason.

**Notes**

1. Joaquin Villalobos, "A Democratic Revolution For El Salvador," *Foreign Policy* 74 (Spring 1989): 107.

Two items of note about this statement and its timing: First, Villalobos is characterized by Radu and Tismaneanu as "more than any other major Salvadoran leader" lacking "scruples, consistency, or personal credibility." (p. 209) Second, this article came out while the FMLN was building up for the November 1989 "Final Offensive", and is thus quite probably part of a propaganda "smokescreen", a tactic learned from the Vietnamese.

2. William Branigan, "Leftists Kill Officials, Civilians, Lifting Salvadoran Toll," *The Washington Post*, 29 August 1988, A20.

Tutela Legal's figures were 24 death squad and 29 FMLN murders. Compare these with the Embassy figures, and the problem of reliable determination of such statistics comes into focus.

3. Branigan, A20.

4. Robert S. Leiken, "The Salvadoran Left," *Central America - Anatomy of a Conflict* (Elmsford NY: Pergamon Press, 1984), 121-122.

5. Clements, 150-157.

"Pedro" may not even have been Salvadoran. He was an "internationalist" mercenary who claimed to be from Costa Rica and to have spent time with the "companeros" in Nicaragua.

6. Chris Hedges, "Rebels terrorize local officials in El Salvador," *Dallas* (Tex.) *Morning News*, 12 May 1985, NEWSBANK 1985 INT 42:F8-9.

7. Douglas Farah, "El Salvador's Mayors Quit in Droves," *The Washington Post*, 8 January 1989, A1.

8. Joaquin Villalobos, "A Democratic Revolution For El Salvador," *Foreign Policy* 74 (Spring 1989): 112.

9. Dr. Terry Karl, telephone interview by writer, 17 April 1991.

Disruption of the March 1991 elections was milder than usual, in that the FMLN seems to have contented itself with a boycott. Several leftist parties did participate, with (for them) encouraging results.

10. Clements, 58.

11. *Statistical Abstract of Latin America*, Vol. 29, p. 292 Table 1060.
Voter absenteeism in the 1982 Constituent Assembly elections was 26.5%, while that in the 1989 Presidential election was 67.4%.

12. "The El Salvador Horror," *The New Republic*, 11 December 1989, 8.

13. Charles Lane, "The War That Will Not End," *The New Republic*, 16 October 1989, 26.

14. *Statistical Abstract of Latin America*, Vol. 29, Table 1058, 292.

15. "D.C. Demonstrators Protest El Salvador Election," *The Washington Post*, 20 March 1989, A27.
This was repeated in a letter from the Nebraska Peace PAC to Representative Peter Hoagland (D-NE), 6 October 1990.
The Nebraska Peace PAC was organized by members of the local CISPES affiliate, among others.

16. Joaquin Villalobos, "A Democratic Revolution For El Salvador," *Foreign Policy* 74 (Spring 1989), 110.

17. "The El Salvador Horror," *The New Republic*, 11 December 1989, 8.

18. "The El Salvador Horror," The New Republic, December 11, 1989, 8.

19. ONUSAL survey, quoted in Embassy of El Salvador letter dated 23 April 1993.
This further breaks down the supporters into 15,000 union members and 23,810 "repatriados."

20. *Statistical Abstract of Latin America*, Vol. 29, Table 1059, 292.

21. Branigan, A20.

22. Robert J. McCartney, "Gunmen Seen Singling Out U.S. Marines," *The Washington Post*, 21 June 1985, A1.

23. "Marines 1st Targets of Salva Massacre Thugs," *New York* (N.Y.) *Post*, 21 June 1985, NEWSBANK, 1985 INT 59:E1.

24. Radio Venceramos, June 21, 1985, reported in June 24 FBIS *Latin America Daily Report*, as quoted by J. Michael Waller, 227.

25. Reuter News Agency report, appended to "Shift in El Salvador Signals War Near End," *The Washington Post*, 5 May 1991, A36.
Confirmed by Consul of El Salvador in San Francisco, CA, telephone interview with writer, 12 June 1991.
Life imprisonment is the maximum sentence under Salvadoran law.

26. President Jose Napoleon Duarte, *Duarte: My Story* (New York: G.P. Putnam's Sons, 1986), 243-267.
Her driver was shot to death and her bodyguard was seriously wounded in the kidnap. And as usual, the FMLN started making other demands as soon as they decided Duarte was serious about negotiating. They offered to free 25 kidnapped mayors in exchange for 29 noncombatant rebel support network personnel. This gives some indication of the scale of the FMLN's terror campaign against local Salvadoran elected officials.

27. CISPES editorial, *Alert!*, July-August 1985, 2.
As quoted by Waller, 227.

28. Sister Marlene Bertke, Pax Christi spokesperson, telephone interview 15 February 1993.

29. Greg Walker, "SOF in El Salvador: The Untold War," *Behind The Lines*, January/February 1992, 16.
"SOF" stands for Special Operations Forces. Mr. Walker's total of fifteen apparently includes all military personnel who died in El Salvador. Of these, seven were assassinated and two killed in action by the FMLN.
Associated Press, "U.S. Citizens Killed in El Salvador," *The Washington Post*, 4 January 1991, A12.
Six U.S. military personnel died in a helicopter accident in July 1987, and four "CIA" employees were killed in the crash of a light reconnaissance aircraft on 19 October 1984. Three more deaths are war-related, including one photographer killed in a crossfire in March 1984, and two murders which have never been solved, but appear to have had a political connection.

30. McNeil, 105.

31. McNeil, 105.

32. House 100-42, 15.

33. House 100-42, 24-25.

34. House 100-42, 25.

35. Americas Watch, *Third Supplement to the Report on Human Rights in El Salvador*, July 19 1983, 65.
   As reprinted in: Senate Committee on Foreign Relations, *Central American Policy: hearing before the Committee on Foreign Relations, United States Senate, Ninety-eighth Congress, first session, on progress on certification in El Salvador, August 4, 1983*, 98-289 (Washington DC: Government Printing Office, 1983), 184.

36. House 100-42, 25-26.

37. House 100-42, 26.

38. "Operational Modes We Will Use," 358.

39. "Operational Modes We Will Use," 358.

40. *The Miami Herald*, "Salvadorans Strive For Enduring Peace," *Omaha World-Herald*, 19 January 1992, 16-A.

41. Lee Hockstadter, "Salvadoran Rebels' Power Play," *The Washington Post*, 27 May 1991, A20.

42. Hockstadter, A20.

43. Hockstadter, A20.

44. Guevara, 63-64.

45. MAJ James K. Waters, "Countermine Operations in El Salvador," *Engineer*, no. 1, 1987, 30.
   As quoted by MAJ Victor M. Rosello, "Vietnam's Support to El Salvador's FMLN," *Military Review*, January 1990, 73.

46. Rosello, 73.

47. Tammy Arbuckle, "El Salvador: The Real War in Central America?" *International Defense Review*, February 1989, 157.

48. Arbuckle, 157.

49. "The El Salvador Horror," 8.

50. Clements, 146.
There is an odd impression from Clements' account that he considered the death to be the Salvadoran Army's fault, on the grounds that the mine had been *intended* for soldiers.

51. Walker, 15.

Chapter 9

# Did CISPES Believe in Human Rights?

CISPES members (and those of other network components) certainly knew that their donations were going to the FMLN, but did they know about the FMLN's terror campaigns? It appears that they must have. Even if they ignored or discounted mainstream press reports of FMLN atrocities, there were accounts available in alternative publications. An Americas Watch report on El Salvador dated July 19, 1983, contains a chapter titled "Human Rights Violations by the Guerrillas," which discusses (among other things) political murders by the FMLN.[1] There was an entire Americas Watch report titled *Violation of Fair Trial Guarantees by the FMLN's Ad Hoc Courts*, which came out in May, 1990. Probably the most damning proof that CISPES and other groups knew - and even approved - of the FMLN's political murder campaigns comes from the "War of the Mayors" in 1988-1989.

This activity was reported in several publications widely circulated among the FMLN support networks, such as *FOCUS* and *Latinamerica Press*. In *FOCUS* the campaign was justified by the statement that "Most of the mayors have been members or supporters of the rightist ARENA party."[2] The article in the *Latinamerica Press* went even farther, gloating that the campaign was a "brilliant move" to counter the counterinsurgency strategy employed by the government.

The guerrillas' successful campaign against the country's mayors is leaving much of El Salvador without a functioning local government and is a major setback for the U.S. strategy to defeat the leftist rebels.[3]

Clearly, at least the 'core' members knew about the FMLN's terroristic activities. It also seems apparent that their views on political murder were conditioned by the political affiliations of the murderers and their victims.

It may be charitable to assume that the members of CISPES and other FMLN sympathizers operated wearing ideological blinders, seeing the situation without regard to context or conflicting evidence. If not, then the classic and discredited 'the ends justify the means' argument appears to have been at work. Their calls for 'peace' and 'human rights' in El Salvador were compromised by their support for the FMLN, a violent and proven violator of those rights. Their support for the FMLN in the name of 'the People' and 'democracy,' despite the FMLN's violent antipathy to the basic forms of democracy and elections showing their political base to be thin, betrays that approach to be bogus as well. Their own partisan dabbling in internal Salvadoran politics negates their stance of 'non-intervention.'

From the evidence it appears that they were not objectively dedicated to any ideals of peace, human rights and democracy, but merely to the advancement of an ideologically congenial political movement - at whatever the cost to the Salvadoran people or even to their own country's interests - in El Salvador. The issues mentioned above were nothing to them but tools to be used to cynically manipulate people, just means to an end.

Official U.S. policy was to objectively denounce terrorism, and condemned that of both the right and of the left. CISPES' denunciation of terrorism was more selective, tending to excuse that of the left. How can such an attitude be supported? Part of the answer is suggested by Gabriel Zaid's eulogy to Roque Dalton; a look into the mind of a revolutionary.

> For Dalton, the errors and horrors of Stalin were supportable - unconditionally acceptable as part of something positive and upward. What he did not wish to accept but rather violently reject was his being bourgeois. The open-mindedness of a progressive bourgeois was to be rejected as insufficient or as stealing from the proletariat. The least little thing that smacked of fascism (and what is there that hasn't smacked of fascism?) was as fascist as Hitler's crimes. A slaughter of innocents carried out by Hitler is in the evil, the sinister, the negative column; a slaughter of innocents carried out by Stalin is in the good, the upwardly positive column. Killing the Chief of Police is the highest achievement for a writer who truly wants to be a revolutionary. To write social criticism, form cultural brigades, put one's pen at the service of the first-class revolutionaries, while eating three meals a day, is for poor slobs who don't dare to take up arms.[4]

As shown earlier, many of the people supporting the Salvadoran revolutionaries (such as Dalton) were armchair revolutionaries themselves. How could an American, coming from a democratic society and considering him- or herself to be politically 'liberal,' support such a murderous movement in the name of 'human rights?' Evidently Morgenthau's "phobic Anti-Americanism" is not confined to non-Americans, as Richard West discovered during his visit to Nicaragua in 1988.

> In the sweltering dining place of the Seven Seas, a US professor of history drinks warm Pepsi Cola (he fears the germs in the ice) and recounts the iniquities of William Walker, 'That was one mean son-of-a-bitch and I'm telling you, you've got to admire the Nicaraguans the way they even speak to us, let alone act so goddam kind to Americans, after the way we've screwed them up.' His listeners murmur 'that's right ... goddam it,' expressing the shame they feel over what their country has done to Nicaragua. They have pale, spectacled, sweaty faces, and bitter smiles that reveal their rather enjoyable guilt over the perfidy of Washington. ... Debate is reduced to a scream of hatred against the United States, and much of it screamed by Americans.
> These Anti-United States Americans are just as troubling in their way as anti-Semitic Jews. ...[5]

A Cuban visitor to the U.S. was shocked by this attitude. In *Driving Through Cuba,* Carlos Gebler told of Father Xavier, who in 1986 visited the U.S. after a trip to Rome.

> He had stayed there in a house with several young American priests. One evening at supper, Xavier noticed a serving mat which was a facsimile of the US coat of arms. There was an eagle and the motto, 'In God We Trust'.
>
> 'How strange,' he said, 'to use the emblem of a nation as a rest for hot plates.'
>
> 'Watch this, then,' said one of the priests. He dropped the mat on the floor and stamped on it. 'This is what I think of the state, the Presidency, Congress and Capitol Hill, the American dream, Uncle Sam and everything else.'
>
> 'I was shocked,' said Father Xavier, ... 'No one would do this in Cuba. Everyone loves their country and the flag, even if they hate the state. The flag stands not for the government, or communism, but for the land, the nation, us.'[6]

This mindset is not only clearly outside the 'mainstream' of American politics, but actually antipathetic to that current of thought and inimical to the society from which it comes. That those representing this view became so influential in this aspect of national debate is a tribute to American adherence to the democratic ideal of free speech, and at the same time deeply disturbing. To have our national policy dictated by overt enemies of our nation flies in the face of all common sense. To put it mildly, they do not have the best interests of the United States at heart. And it seems clear that they did have some effect, at least in the news media and in Congress.

### Notes

1. This report is reprinted in Senate 98-289, pp. 183-184.

2. "El Salvador," *FOCUS On Central America*, pub. Intercommunity Center for Justice and Peace, February, 1989, 1.

3. Chris Norton, "Massive resignation of Salvadoran mayors undercuts U.S. strategy," *Latinamerica Press*, January 26, 1989, 1.

4. Gabriel Zaid, "The Dalton Affair", *The Central American Crisis Reader*, ed. Robert S. Leiken & Barry Rubin (New York: Summit Books, 1987), 362-363.

5. Richard West, *Hurricane in Nicaragua* (London: Michael Joseph, 1989), 28.

6. Carlo Gebler, *Driving Through Cuba* (New York: Simon and Schuster, 1988), 281-282.

Chapter 10

# The Media and Congress

As stated earlier, one of the strategic goals of the FMLN and its U.S. support network in the 'War of Information' was to force a complete cutoff of U.S. aid to the Salvadoran government. The targets in this conflict were the disseminators of information - the national news media - and Congress. This strategic goal was never quite met, but the FMLN did succeed in developing a significant amount of influence with the major U.S. news media and in Congress.

**The 1989 FMLN Offensive in the News**

Karen DeYoung, while working for the *Washington Post*, once said that "most journalists now, most Western journalists at least, are very eager to seek out guerrilla groups, leftist groups, because you assume they must be the good guys . . ."[1] Certainly not all U.S. journalists (not even all *Washington Post* reporters) would subscribe to Ms. DeYoung's statement. But taken as a whole, a definite slant is evident in the U.S. news media's handling of the war in El Salvador. The Media Research Center has conducted a number of studies of such bias, and their examination of the news coverage of the FMLN's 1989 'Final Offensive' is illuminating.

- Most reporters portrayed alleged right-wing assassinations as more important than FMLN killings. Newscasts and newspapers were dominated by the murders of six Jesuits by "right-wing" elements. Only one story contrasted the Jesuit killings with the continuing campaign of assassinations of government officials by the FMLN.

- The news outlets described the right as "extreme" but never the left. In the twenty days of coverage, not one reporter identified the FMLN as "communist," but simply as "leftist" (123 times) or "Marxist-led" (20 times). But reporters continually used terms such as "extreme right" and "far right" to describe the other side.

- The media rarely (only five times) referred to Cristiani's government as "democratic" or "freely elected." And they never described the FMLN insurgency as "undemocratic."[2]

This leftward tilt of the major U.S. news media made itself apparent during the 1989 offensive, but didn't become an embarrassment until the Nicaraguan elections the following year. As Robert Leiken noted, the defeat of the Sandinistas in the 1990 elections took the media by surprise, since "practically every American pollster, pundit, news organization, and Latin American expert felt certain the Sandinistas would win by a large margin."[3] Stephen Schwartz analyzed this partisanship in his book *A Strange Silence*.

- Ninety-two percent of U.S. coverage of the Sandinista campaign described the Sandinistas as holding the lead. Sixty percent of reportage on the UNO campaign said UNO was trailing. Sixty percent of the U.S. sample predicted a Sandinista win.

- Seventy-six percent of U.S. analysis of UNO was critical or otherwise negative toward the Chamorro candidacy.

- Despite the high inflation rate and other economic problems the country faced, only 5 percent of U.S. coverage before the vote dealt with the economy.

- Fully one-third of all U.S. coverage of the election dealt with U.S.-Nicaraguan relations, contra policy, and U.S. reaction to the vote.

- . . . .

- . . . .

- U.S. media published twice as many interviews with Ortega as with Chamorro, while Canadian media published one-third more with Ortega than with Chamorro.[4]

Since historically supporters of the Sandinistas tended also to support the FMLN, and the election debacle showed how slanted and wrong the media was about Nicaragua, this at least suggests that the media may have had a similar bias about El Salvador. Part of the problem may be that world events are too complex for all of it to be encapsulated and processed for public consumption, thus journalists must pick and choose what they will report. This is combined with the very human tendency for journalists to cover stories that attract their interest, and to approach them from a congenial direction. Thus it can be expected that many otherwise newsworthy stories will not make it through the filter and become 'news.' How else can one explain the major news media completely ignoring such a story as Congressional support for left-wing anti-American terrorists?

## Congress

In Congress the primary targets of the pro-FMLN networks were not, as might be expected, conservative Republicans. Instead the networks concentrated on those they saw as basically sympathetic and thus most vulnerable to influence; liberal Democrats.

> . . . [C]onservatives such as Mr. Hyde are not the targets of the left's lobbying campaign. Instead, it is liberal Democrats, such as Sen. Christopher Dodd of Connecticut and Sen. John Kerry of Massachusetts, who oppose the administration's Central America policy but refuse to vote to end military aid to El Salvador.

About 100 protesters occupied Mr. Kerry's district offices in Boston on Nov. 14 to demand that he oppose aid to the Salvadoran government. A coalition of groups, including CISPES' Boston affiliate and the Central America Solidarity Association, joined in the sit-in, which resulted in 14 arrests.[5]

A number of Congressional liberals were never subject to this kind of harassment. The reason is quite simple. They, themselves, were part of the pro-FMLN networks.

It cannot be said that everyone in Congress who at various times, for various reasons, voted against or tried to set conditions on aid to the Salvadoran government was under the sway of the FMLN/FDR. Nevertheless, it appears that the FMLN/FDR did develop a significant amount of influence, evidence of which surfaced in the aftermath of the Six Jesuits murder.

> In Congress, some have long been skeptical of Salvadoran government efforts to halt the political killings, and others actually have desired that the guerrillas take power. Assigning blame for the killings without proof and aiming to punish the Cristiani government for them, they wasted no time in calling for an immediate halt to U.S. aid.[6]

This faction was amazingly successful in shedding criticism. One of them, Patricia Schroeder, coined the term 'teflon Presidency' to apply to President Reagan. It appears that she and her colleagues may have had a thick coating themselves. Rather like the sacred cattle of India, they seemed to be able to blunder about without interference from either the Congressional leadership or the press.

A distinguishing feature of the members of this faction was not necessarily their voting record, but their willingness to cross the line, to go beyond the accepted bounds of the political arena. Thus members of the United States Congress carried their opposition to President Ronald Reagan's Central American policy beyond the accepted norms of policy disagreement - voting, expressing dissent, proposing counter-legislation, etc. - into the realm of actual support for the other side. This other side was, of course, the FMLN, which we have seen was a virulently anti-American organization with a totalitarian

Marxist ideology, which considered itself to be at war with the United States.

According to J. Michael Waller's *The Third Current of Revolution*, ten members of Congress actually endorsed CISPES fundraising activities. As for other FMLN-connected networks, twenty-one supported Medical Aid for El Salvador (MAES), three endorsed New El Salvador Today (NEST), four were involved with the Salvadoran Humanitarian Aid, Research, and Education Foundation (SHARE), and nineteen worked with FMLN-associated Sister City projects. There was actually a certain amount of overlap, an extreme example being Ronald Dellums (D-CA) who supported four of these organizations.[7]

Even this support is not a completely reliable indication of a seriously pro-FMLN bent, due to the deceptive nature of FMLN network programs (presented under humanitarian disguise) and the reliance on Congressional staffs to do research and draw up correspondence. If, however, this association continued over a long period of time and embraced related groups, such as other 'solidarity' organizations, it is a strong indicator that the member of Congress had come to identify with the FMLN's cause. Somewhere along the line the actual goals of the networks should have become obvious, especially since members of Congress have access to classified intelligence.

This leads to a secondary but strikingly common characteristic of FMLN supporters, and has to do with their relationship with the U.S. intelligence community. This may be broken down into two parts:

1. Active hostility towards U.S. intelligence, counterintelligence, and even counterterrorism operations, coupled with a tendency to denigrate or ignore intelligence reports.

2. Acceptance and active promotion of radical left and Soviet-bloc propaganda and disinformation.

To discuss each member in detail would take a great deal of time and space. With this in mind, two examples will be presented, each with both representative and singular characteristics; Ron Dellums and Patricia Schroeder.

### Ronald Dellums (D-CA)

Ron Dellums was an early supporter of CISPES and the FMLN. During Farid Handal's visit to the United States in 1980 Dellums invited him to address the Black Caucus. Handal duly covered the result in his trip report, which was later captured during a raid on an FMLN safe house in San Salvador.

> Monday morning the offices of Congressman Dellums were turned into our offices. Everything was done there. The meeting with the Black Caucus took place in the liver of the monster itself, nothing less than in the meeting room of the commission of the exterior [House Foreign Affairs]. . . .[8]

On April 22, 1983 the Progressive Hill Staff Group, a creature of Dellums' and John Conyers' (D-MI) staffs, brought three Sandinista officials to the Capitol without the knowledge of the State Department. The Sandinistas' purpose was "to put pressure on the administration by convincing members of Congress to take their part against American policies in Nicaragua."[9] Besides such direct ties with the FMLN and the Sandinistas, Dellums was also closely involved with the Institute of Policy Studies (as a 'special friend') and the World Peace Council,[10] the latter a known Soviet front organization.[11]

Ron Dellums was not really an extremist in this faction. The only exceptional things were his consistency and breadth of activity - he was connected with the international radical left network and had been there since the 1960s. And Dellums is, at the time of this writing, a member of the House Intelligence Committee and the head of the House Armed Services Committee. This is particularly disturbing in light of his association with the IPS, which among its other anti-U.S. intelligence activities has consistently helped and supported Philip Agee, probably the most famous and vicious defector from the CIA in history.[12]

## Patricia Schroeder (D-CO)

Dellums was not alone in these kinds of associations. In May 1981, Patricia Schroeder (D-CO), Don Edwards (D-CA), and John Conyers hosted a delegation from the World Peace Council, and "invited fellow congressmen and staffers 'to meet members of an international delegation . . . led by Romesh Chandra, president of the World Peace Council, to discuss the global impact of arms spending . . . and developments in Central and South America.'"[13] Almost certainly El Salvador was discussed at this forum, and doubtless Schroeder and her colleagues were presented the Soviet party line on "developments in Central and South America." Were they - or more specifically, was she - influenced by this KGB 'active measure?' Subsequent events seem to show that even if there was not direct influence, there was certainly common ground on such issues.

She has had a long and fruitful association with the Institute for Policy Studies, as noted by Steven Powell in *Covert Cadres*. The relationship was so close that when IPS threw a twentieth anniversary celebration to raise funds on April 5, 1983, she was on the committee.[14] It should come as no surprise, then, that she became involved in IPS-associated FMLN support networks. She promoted fundraising for both CISPES and Medical Aid for El Salvador.[15] And she was strategically placed to help CISPES if it needed it, being on the House Armed Services Committee and the Committee on the Judiciary.[16]

Patricia Schroeder has also shown a certain carelessness about the lives of American military and intelligence personnel. She signed a fundraising letter for MAES dated September 16, 1987, two years after MAES' clients (the FMLN) had murdered four Marines and two American civilians in San Salvador. She and her colleagues in the House Subcommittee on Civil and Constitutional Rights - Don Edwards, John Conyers, Robert Kastenmeier (D-WI), and Charles Schumer (D-NY) - voted against the Intelligence Agents Identities Protection Act, "designed to prevent 'Philip Agee types' from publicizing the names of CIA officers and imperiling their lives in the process."[17] This was after Richard Welch, identified by Agee's publication *Counterspy* as a CIA agent, had been assassinated by leftist terrorists in Athens, Greece.[18]

Thus we see a minority faction of 'left-of-liberals' with its powers amplified by strategic placement and its activities unchecked by serious oversight, either through official channels or by the media. And it was very well placed indeed when the FBI initiated an investigation of CISPES and its support for the FMLN/FDR. For the House Committee on the Judiciary served to oversee the activities of the FBI, and its Subcommittee on Civil and Constitutional Rights - dominated by these associates of CISPES and the IPS - investigated this FBI investigation.[19]

### Notes

1. S. Steven Powell, *Covert Cadre: Inside the Institute for Policy Studies* (Ottawa IL: Green Hill Publishers, 1987), 23.

2. L. Brent Bozell III & Brent H. Baker, *And That's The Way It Is(n't)* (Alexandria VA: Media Research Center, 1990), 145-146.

3. Robert S. Leiken, "Oops," *The New Republic*, 19 March 1990, 16.

4. Stephen Schwartz, *A Strange Silence* (San Francisco: Institute for Contemporary Studies, 1992), 131-132.

5. Peter LaBarbera, "Salvador rebels' allies leap into action here," *Washington* (D.C.) *Times*, 24 November 1989, NEWSBANK 1989 INT 123:D4.

6. "Moderation Caught in a Cross Fire," NEWSBANK 1989 INT 135:G6.
This tendency to assign blame and punish without proof appears to be congenital to the group, and is also evident in the House hearings on the FBI investigation of CISPES.

7. Waller, Appendix 13.
A list abstracted from his information with additions from CISPES (and other) literature is in the Appendix.

8. Uri Ra'anan, Robert L. Pfatzgraff, Jr., et al, *Hydra of Carnage: International Linkages of Terrorism and Other Low-Intensity Operations* (Lexington MA: Lexington Books, 1986), 356.

9. Powell, 260.

10. Powell, 263.

11. U.S. Department of State, *Soviet Active Measures: The World Peace Council* (Washington DC: Department of State, 1985).

12. S. Steven Powell, *Covert Cadre: Inside the Institute for Policy Studies* (Ottawa IL: Green Hill Publishers, 1987), 68.

13. Powell, 78.

14. Powell, 249-250.

15. Waller, 273-274.

16. Powell, 250.
House 100-122, III.

17. Powell, 76.

18. Powell, 66.

19. House 100-122, III.

Chapter 11

# The FBI Investigation

The rather garbled media account of the Congressional hearings on the FBI investigation of CISPES gives the impression of the FBI trying to explain a bungled, politically motivated harassment operation along the lines of COINTELPRO, against opponents of U.S. Central American policy guilty of nothing worse than polite dissent.[1] The truth is quite different. After spending almost as much time and money investigating the CISPES investigation as the original operation had cost,[2] it was concluded that nothing illegal had been done by the FBI, (except by one case agent who resigned before the original CISPES investigation had been complete) and that the two main problems had been the unreliability of the primary informant, and the unjustified broadening of the scope of the investigation.[3]

### The Armed Resistance Unit and CISPES

What attracted the FBI's interest to CISPES to begin with was a Justice Department request to investigate CISPES as possibly being in violation of the Foreign Agents Registration Act (FARA). This investigation, running from September 3, 1981 to February 23, 1982, closed with the FBI finding that "[a]lthough there were some 'indications that the money collected by CISPES may be finding its way to the FDR,' the FBI said that it had 'no real substantiated information linking CISPES financially to the FPL/FDR, or proof that CISPES is acting on behalf of or at the direction of the FPL/FDR or any foreign principal'."[4]

This statement is particularly interesting in light of later revelations by CISPES itself that it was providing money and supplies to the FMLN/FDR. Apparently by then CISPES felt immune to official federal scrutiny of its activities. During the hearings Congressman Sensenbrenner tried to ensure that 1) CISPES would not get immunity from investigation such as the Institute of Policy Studies had enjoyed since 1979, and 2) that the 'standards of predication' would not be raised.[5] It should be remembered that double jeopardy only applies to court cases, not to investigations, so CISPES should have been vulnerable to re-investigation.

To continue, in 1983 a series of three bombings was committed in and around Washington, D.C., carried out the same time as a CISPES convention. The organization claiming credit for the attack was the Armed Resistance Unit, also known as the May 19 Communist Organization.[6] In its communique dated April 26, 1983, it stated the following:

> Tonight we attacked Fort Lesley McNair Military base in Washington, D.C. . . . This action was taken in solidarity with the growing liberation movements in El Salvador, in Guatemala, and throughout Central America, and with the socialist government of Nicaragua. This region today is the center of world revolution and the front line in the defeat of U.S. imperialism. . . .
> The courage, sacrifice, and determination of the people of El Salvador is [sic] an inspiration to oppressed people throughout the world. Our action is part of the growing world solidarity with that struggle.[7]

This, combined with information from an expatriate Salvadoran named Frank Varelli, made the FBI decide that it had sufficient cause to initiate an investigate of CISPES under their counterterrorism guidelines. According to a Senate report, "the FBI has the authority to investigate foreign guerrilla movements such as the FMLN and persons in the United States who knowingly assist their terrorist activities."[8] The international terrorism guidelines used were from the Foreign Intelligence Surveillance Act (FISA) of 1978, which defines international terrorism "to mean activities that:"

(1) involve violent acts or acts dangerous to human life that are a violation of the criminal laws of the United States or of any State or that would be a criminal violation if committed within the jurisdiction of the United States or any State;
(2) appear to be intended-
  (A) to intimidate or coerce a civilian population;
  (B) to influence the policy of a government by intimidation or coercion; or
  (C) to affect the conduct of a government by assassination or kidnapping; and
(3) occur totally outside the United States, or transcend national boundaries in terms of the means by which they are carried out, the persons they appear intended to coerce or intimidate, or the locale in which their perpetrators operate or seek asylum.[9]

That there was a fine line to be walked in this investigation was recognized by the FBI, because the FISA also provides that "no U.S. person may be considered a foreign power or an agent of a foreign power solely on the basis of activities protected by the first amendment to the Constitution . . ."[10] Thus a message was sent out cautioning field offices as to the intended scope of the investigation.

It should be noted that many of the members of CISPES and/or its subgroups may not be aware that their fund raising activities, the subsequent funds, and other support which they furnish to CISPES is directed by CISPES officials to support the terroristic activities of the El Salvadoran leftist terrorists. This investigation is not concerned with the exercise of rights guaranteed by the U.S. Constitution, but rather, with the involvement of individuals and the CISPES organization in international terrorism as it affects the El Salvadoran government, and the collection of foreign intelligence and counterintelligence information as it relates to the international terrorism aspects of this investigation. . . .[11]

In October 1983 the scope was broadened, bringing more FBI field offices into it. The instructions "in essence directed all field offices to regard each CISPES chapter, wherever located, as a proper subject of the investigation."[12] By the middle of 1984, however, some doubt began to be cast on Frank Varelli's reliability as an informant. By then "there was other classified information indicating that specific individuals associated with CISPES were engaged in activities that would justify investigation. . . . Those activities would not, however, have justified the investigation of CISPES as an organization."[13] The Senate report goes on to state that the investigation of CISPES as an organization should have been terminated at that point, since the original predicate was no longer valid.

The investigation became a scandal when Frank Varelli went public trying to sue the FBI for back pay as an informant. After an extensive investigation of the investigation, the FBI's director, William Sessions, testified before the Senate.

> Varelli's initial case agent, who resigned from the FBI in 1984, gave Varelli classified documents and withheld money that was to have been paid to Varelli. Other than that, my inspectors have not identified any illegal acts or violations of constitutional rights committed by the FBI as part of the CISPES investigation. They did identify thirty-one instances of possible violations of the Attorney General Guidelines, mostly of a minor and technical nature. Since that time, the Bureau's Legal Counsel Division has opined that only fifteen of these instances were in fact violations, and that of these violations, thirteen warrant being reported to the President's Intelligence Oversight Board.
> . . .[C]ontrary to certain allegations, the CISPES investigation was not a return to the days of COINTELPRO. As initially conceived, the investigation was a reasonable examination of a terrorist threat. That its execution was flawed reflects mismanagement. It does not reflect a policy of purposeful interference with legitimate domestic political activity.[14]

As for a 'White House Connection' in the investigation, no evidence to support this allegation has ever surfaced. On the contrary, William Sessions testified that:

> There is no evidence that the White House or anyone acting on behalf of the White House gave instructions, requested information, or otherwise attempted to influence the CISPES investigation. The same is true of all other government agencies and

outside private groups. There is no evidence that the CISPES investigation was politically motivated or directed.[15]

## The Congressional Inquisition into the FBI Investigation of CISPES

The Senate hearings, to their credit, seem to have adhered to technical and legal matters and are largely free of cant (with the exception of Senator Howard M. Metzenbaum, D-OH). The House hearings, however, are in sharp contrast. The House committee which investigated was the Subcommittee on Civil and Constitutional Rights of the Committee on the Judiciary. It was packed with CISPES supporters and chaired by Don Edwards (D-CA), a man with close contacts with the Institute for Policy Studies and the World Peace Council.[16] Besides their history of hostility toward the U.S. intelligence community, the Reagan administration, and official Central American policy, there was something personal. Pat Schroeder (D-CO) thought she had been investigated by the FBI for her ties to the FMLN and Sandinistas, based on a forged FBI file page which had been leaked to the press by Varelli.[17] That she was allowed to attack the FBI's investigation as a member of the committee strikes one as something of a conflict of interest; she was clearly not impartial.[18] But then, neither were three of her cohorts. Charles Schumer (D-NY) was, like Edwards, connected with the Institute of Policy Studies, John Conyers (D-MI) was an overt supporter of MAES and NEST, and Robert Kastenmeier (D-WI) was involved with the Madison, Wisconsin - Arcatao, Chalatenango (in an FMLN controlled zone) Sister City project. Only three other House members were on the committee, and they were largely overshadowed by their colleagues, with the single voice of reason coming from F. James Sensenbrenner, Jr. (R-WI).

Thus the tone of the House report is hostile, and the questioning sometimes verges on the vicious. Congressmen Conyers wondered why CISPES was being investigated while "[o]ne of the most embarrassing parts of the FBI is that the Klan is very, very poorly investigated, very little investigation."[19] He more than hinted at an ideological bias in the FBI.

This charge is ludicrous. The Ku Klux Klan is a small, discredited, politically marginal group which has been thoroughly investigated by many agencies, including the FBI, and which steadily declined in strength and influence throughout the 1980s.[20] Its presumed 'international' contact was the Skinheads, which connection Conyers claimed to exist "according to today's New York Times article on the Skinheads, that now show them in contact with at least certain leadership within the Klan . . ."[21] That this tenuous link constituted reasonable grounds for investigation under international terrorism guidelines, while CISPES's cuddly association with the FMLN did not, reveals more about Conyer's ideological preoccupations than the FBI's.[22]

While castigating the FBI, Conyers praised the success of private groups in investigating the Ku Klux Klan. This brings up the matter of 'private spying.' Such activity was commendable when the target was the KKK, but Schroeder expressed a great deal of concern over what she called "information vigilantes" who might be prying into CISPES activities and giving the results to the FBI.

> MRS. SCHROEDER. So if groups of people decided to go gather information on their own, information vigilantes, and they got information and brought it to law enforcement officials, it would be okay for law enforcement officials to use it and it would not be considered law enforcement involvement; is that what I hear you saying?[23]

Schroeder was concerned that the FBI investigation might have been "privatized," and was clearly upset about it. Similar concern was expressed by Senator Metzenbaum in the Senate hearings, to such a degree that he considered involvement by a private conservative organization in obtaining the Farid Handal travel notes to have discredited the documents completely.[24] Yet one of the witnesses at the 1987 House hearings was Lindsay Mattison, Director of the International Center for Development Policy, who boasted of the ICDP's Commission on United States-Latin American Relations (headed by former Ambassador Robert White), which appears to have been nothing but a left-wing 'information vigilante' group engaged in 'private spying.'

> Our delegations provide a constant stream of knowledgeable witnesses before the committees of the House and Senate. And, more than once, our delegations have produced revelations in the press and in Congress of the CIA's role in organizing the

Contras against Nicaragua [sic], of Roberto D'Aubuisson's part in the death squad killings in El Salvador, and more recently, of the Reagan Administration's violation of the Boland Amendment and other U.S. laws by a covert National Security Council effort to aid the Contras [sic].[25]

Far from being censured by the House subcommittee, Mattison was treated with great respect. It appears, then, that the determination of whether or not a group was engaged in 'information vigilantism' was based on how closely its politics and aims matched that of the Congressional liberals dominating the committees. This was not the only time during the hearings when partisan politics was used to set standards.

Both Conyers and Kastenmeier pushed a view that the CISPES investigation was politically motivated and directed against opponents of Reagan's Central American policy. FBI Director William Sessions' testimony specifically refuted this charge. The Congressmen tried to compare the FMLN with the Nicaraguan Resistance, claiming that special treatment had been given to the latter and its supporters, and that there wasn't any substantial difference between the two groups.[26]

> CONYERS: How do we get to the decision that the FMLN becomes a terrorist organization, while the contras are not a terrorist organization. Both are rebel groups within their own country.[27]

The big difference, as we have seen (and as pointed out by FBI Director Sessions), is that the FMLN specifically "directed bombings and assassination plots against U.S. persons [killing at least fourteen] and U.S. interests."[28] Despite a great deal of publicity and a deliberate program of 'witnesses' trying to put themselves in the line of fire to protect the Sandinistas, the contras killed one: Benjamin Linder.

Support for the contras was also national policy, while support for the FMLN ran directly counter to that policy, a fact which received no attention during the hearings. There is even an impression gathered from Kastenmeier that the official policy was "Administration" policy, and thus little better than opinion.

> I think what he [Conyers] was driving at [is] there appears to be a differentiation between groups the Administration would regard politically as terrorists, and then those other groups operating in other countries that are more consistent with the foreign policy position that the country is taking or the Administration is taking, and therefore, puts the standards in a different category.[29]

This is a very revealing statement. In it, the FMLN, despite having declared itself at war with the U.S., becomes just another guerrilla group operating in another country. Apparently, in Conyers' and Kastenmeier's view, attacks on American interests and loss of American life did not an enemy make. The official policy of the United States was also dismissed as a criterion by which to judge the FMLN as terrorist. Clearly, U.S. policy was not recognized by Kastenmeier and his associates. It thus becomes fair to ask, what policy did they recognize, and whose side were they on? Their defense of the FMLN support networks suggests an obvious answer.

Perhaps the primary lesson the FBI learned, therefore, was political rather than technical. It is dangerous to investigate groups, however dubious, when they are connected with and thus protected by members of the dominant party in Congress. The expense and labor of investigating the investigation, plus the 'show trials' before a hostile House subcommittee, had a definite chilling effect. The message transmitted was that there are things to be left alone, at whatever the cost to U.S. national interests, if the trail leads to the liberal 'sacred cattle' of Congress.

**Liberal Coverup?**

There is no direct evidence that a conspiracy to cover up Congressional involvement with the FMLN support networks took place. There is, on the other hand, considerable circumstantial evidence that the House hearings on the CISPES investigation were politically motivated, and that CISPES was granted de facto immunity from investigation and prosecution, largely because such activities would prove politically embarrassing to the Democratic Party. At the very least Congressional behavior during the hearings suggests that a

## The FBI Investigation

double standard (with teeth) was at work. In the absence of hard evidence (memos or tapes indicating a conspiracy) what follows is informed speculation. Events seem to have been shaped by these factors:

1. All (except 'democratic socialist' Bernie Sanders of Vermont) of the Congressional FMLN support network endorsers were liberal Democrats, mostly in the House of Representatives.

2. Some were under investigation by the FBI because of their links with the FMLN and the Sandinistas, while others thought they were because of information leaked by Frank Varelli - information later proved to be unreliable.

3. Congressional ties to the support networks couldn't be denied, because there were too many letters in circulation with embarrassing signatures.

The effort for dealing with the crisis seems to have focused on two general areas:

1. The FMLN/FDR had to be presented in as benevolent a light as possible, and the networks had to be whitewashed and delinked from it.

2. The FBI investigation had to be discredited, and further investigation had to be prevented. That there were some problems with the FBI's handling of the case just made it easier.

Kastenmeier's and Conyers' attempt to 'neutralize' the FMLN, by identifying it as equivalent to the Nicaraguan Resistance, has been remarked. There was also a curious difference between the House subcommittee's fundamental attitude and that evident in the Senate's Intelligence Committee reports. The Senate's primary concern (aside from the histrionics of Senator Metzenbaum) was with the flawed management of the CISPES investigation, while the House was much more particular. Subcommittee Chairman Don Edwards commented on the first page of the House report that ". . . [M]any Americans would be surprised to learn that the FBI does not have to focus on criminal activity when it is dealing with international terrorism."³⁰ Since kidnapping and assassination are clearly criminal activities, one can only conclude that what Edwards was trying to put across was that if CISPES or the FMLN had been conducting these overtly criminal activities within the United States, then and only then would the investigation have been justified. In other words, support for terrorism - even terrorism against Americans - was all right so long as that terrorism was conducted abroad.

As we've seen, even this approach does not completely exonerate CISPES. The Communist Party USA helped found the organization, and CISPES conducted activities in coordination with other known U.S. terrorist groups; for example, the Prairie Fire Organizing Committee raised money for the CISPES-administered Bravo Fund. CISPES was part of the support committee for the Armed Resistance bombers, and if it didn't actually order the bombings appears to have been an influence, as evidenced by the bombers' statements being almost identical in wording with CISPES pronouncements.³¹ It printed inflammatory propaganda and frequently engaged in illegal activities, mostly of a minor nature.³² However, at least one of its members actually took up arms against the elected government of El Salvador and its chief ally, her own country; an unambiguous act of treason. Others had dual membership with the FMLN, and some were investigated by the FBI for felonies, which appear to have included domestic terrorism and arms smuggling.³³

This approach does, however, appear to be part of a pattern of attempting to push all of CISPES' most unsavory activities out of the country, back onto the FMLN/FDR. And once exiled, in order to whitewash CISPES and thus to preserve the reputations of those in Congress supporting it, the connection had to be severed. Thus the testimony of CISPES national program coordinator Michael Lent, that no link existed between CISPES and the FMLN/FDR, was seriously questioned only by Congressman Sensenbrenner and Counsel Slobodin.

> During the hearing, Sensenbrenner and minority counsel Alan Slobodin closely questioned Michael Lent of CISPES, seeking to link his group to the Farabundo Marti National Liberation Front and its political arm, the Democratic Revolutionary Front (-FMLN/FDR). Lent, who denied any link to the Salvadoran

rebel-political-military coalition,[italics mine] said the FBI had been investigating his organization for six years, attempting to "discredit" it by raising "questions and doubts about where money collected nationally for humanitarian aid was actually going."[34]

Compare the statement that CISPES had no "link to the Salvadoran rebel-political-military coalition" with that of Van Gosse, also a CISPES national staff member, but this time writing in the book *Reshaping the US Left*, published in 1988. In the early 1980's, as both CISPES and the FMLN were forming, the older U.S. leftist groups "were . . . suspicious of the close connection between Salvadorans from the BPR and much of the CISPES leadership."[35]

> For the latter, political and personal ties with the people you are 'in solidarity with' were nothing to be ashamed of. Among the Salvadorans one tendency had emphasized North American solidarity early and often [the FPL], and therefore had the strongest relations with the North Americans. This contributed to tensions with the Salvadorans aligned with the other organizations of the FMLN/FDR . . . but CISPES simply shrugged off its uneven relation to these groups.[36]

It thus seems clear that very close "links" existed between CISPES and the FMLN/FDR. It also appears that Michael Lent perjured himself before the House subcommittee. That this lie was allowed to stand suggests that some sort of immunity was granted to CISPES by its Congressional supporters. As to the second part of Michael Lent's testimony, the complaint that the FBI was trying to cast doubt on where CISPES' 'humanitarian' aid was going, as we have seen in earlier chapters there is every reason for legitimate suspicion.

Evidence that further investigation was not to be tolerated comes from Independent Counsel Lawrence Walsh's probe of Iran-Contra. His mandate as finally approved was quite broad, covering a) arms sales to Iran, and b) support for the Nicaraguan Resistance during the Boland Amendment period. Little known is that Representative Henry Hyde (R-IL) proposed that it include investigation of the FMLN support networks.

> Rep. Henry Hyde yesterday urged that the investigation of the Iran-Contra episode include allegations that money meant for

humanitarian aid in El Salvador was diverted to Marxist guerrillas in that country.
The Illinois Republican proposed petitioning the three-judge panel that chose Lawrence E. Walsh as independent counsel to include any diversion of aid to the Marxist rebels in El Salvador as part of the special investigation.[37]

This proposal never reached the Court, and doesn't appear to have made it out of Congress. Considering the involvement of Democrats almost exclusively in the FMLN networks, this would tend to confirm the view that the Iran-Contra probe became a partisan political weapon to use against the Republican administration. For many U.S. citizens (including some in Congress), the three main problems with Iran-Contra were 1) arms being provided to Iran, our self-declared enemy, 2) the dubious legality and morality of defying the law by 'privatizing' Contra aid, and 3) lying about it to Congress.[38] An examination of similar activities conducted by Congressional Democrats would only seem reasonable. Yet official FBI inquiry into the private aid operation for the FMLN in El Salvador - another self-declared enemy of the United States - was suppressed, and the chief spokesman for that private aid organization lied to Congress with no repercussions whatever.

In the more recent 'Iraq-Gate' one of the primary questions asked was: Who knew about the loans going to Iraq before the U.S. and its allies went to war with Saddam Hussein? There has never been any comparable question raised about funding going to the FMLN *while* it was at war with the United States.

To sum up, it appears that the pro-CISPES clique in Congress deliberately used private networks to undermine official policy, assisted in funding a guerrilla war against a U.S. ally, and used their official positions to protect a support network for anti-American terrorists. Their motivation for the last, far from any sort of idealism about civil rights, appears to have been primarily to protect their own political careers from the consequences of their other actions. Actions which most of their constituents (with the probable exception of Dellums') would find repellent if the truth was revealed.

## Notes

1. "The FBI's Sorry Story", *TIME*, April 29, 1988, 42.

2. Senate 100-1051, 130.

3. Senate 100-1051, 90.

4. Senate 100-1051, 20-22.

5. House 100-122, 161.

6. This group is the East Coast branch of the Prairie Fire Organizing Committee(PFOC), itself an outgrowth of the Weathermen. The West Coast PFOC had direct contact with the FMLN (in 1991) through its representative Luis Flores, and raised money for the CISPES-administered Bravo Fund.

7. Senate Select Committee on Intelligence, *Senate Select Committee on Intelligence inquiry into the FBI investigation of the Committee in Solidarity with the People of El Salvador (CISPES)*, 101-46, (Washington DC: Government Printing Office, 1989), 135.

8. Senate 101-46, 92.

9. Senate 101-46, 92.

10. Senate 101-46, 92.

11. Senate 101-46, 29.

12. Senate 100-1051, 122.

13. Senate 101-46, 90.

14. Senate 100-1051, 123.

15. Senate 100-1051, 122.

16. IPS member Isabel Letelier helped found CISPES, and among IPS's spinoffs is Policy Alternatives for the Caribbean and Central America (PACCA), another leftist pressure group with a Latin American focus.

17. This appears to have been a forgery by Varelli using a copy of an actual FBI form.

18. It is not much of a stretch to compare this with the idea of LtCol Oliver North being appointed to investigate the Iran-Contra probe. Schroeder clearly did not believe Director Sessions' testimony that she had not been investigated, as evidenced by her correspondence on the subject appended to House document 100-42, pp. 656-660, and her comment about being burglarized by FBI informants during the 1970s, p. 396.

19. House 100-122, 110.

20. Anti-Defamation League of B'nai B'rith (ADL), *The KKK Today: A 1991 Status Report* (New York: Civil Rights Division of the Anti-Defamation League of B'nai B'rith, 1991), 1.

This report places KKK membership in 1987-1988 as "4,500 to 5,500" and declining, for several reasons. Two of the more significant of these were: 1) active investigation of KKK involvement in violence, followed by "convictions and stiff sentences given the participants. . . ." and 2) the economic prosperity of Reagan/Bush administrations, because of which the KKK (and other extremists) were unable "to mobilize significant protest movements against what were generally perceived to be good times, both at home and abroad."

According to another ADL publication, in 1983 and 1984 an attempt at a "violent revolution against the American government" by the Aryan Resistance Movement "was aborted by the prompt and effective response of the FBI, the Treasury Department's Bureau of Alcohol, Tobacco and Firearms, and other law enforcement agencies."

Anti-Defamation League of B'nai B'rith, *Hate Groups in America: A Record of Bigotry and Violence* (New York: Anti-Defamation League of B'nai B'rith, 1988), 41.

21. House 100-122, 111.

22. This is not to imply that the KKK and similar groups do not bear watching. The ADL publications cited above were used because the ADL was considered a reliable source of such statistics by individuals in the FBI, the Omaha Police Department, and by Klanwatch.

23. House 100-42, 383.

24. Senate 101-46, 69.

25. House 100-42, 96-97.
At least two statements in this paragraph are incorrect. The Contras were organized against the Sandinistas, not against their own country. Strictly speaking, the Boland Amendment was never violated by the NSC because the NSC was exempt from its provisions.

26. House 100-122, 157-158.

27. House 100-122, 158.

28. House 100-122, 158.
Greg Walker, *Behind The Lines*, 15. This gives fifteen as the total U.S. military killed.
The dedication of J. Michael Waller's *The Third Current of Revolution* contains a partial list of 14 names, including five civilians.
Two Americans have been confirmed as killed by the Salvadoran security forces. One was Michael Kline, who died on 13 October 1982 while being taken in for questioning. Three soldiers were tried for his murder. The other was "internationalist" mercenary Carroll Ishee, who joined the FMLN and was KIA in August 1983.

29. House 100-122, 163.

30. House 100-122, 1.

31. Senate 100-1051, 52.
Senate 101-46, 135-138.
The latter are the texts of the bombers' statements.

32. During the Congressional hearings it was revealed that some individual members of CISPES were under investigation for more serious illegal activities, but that there was no evidence that these were being conducted under the direct orders of the CISPES leadership.

33. Rebecca Tarver was certainly carrying a weapon in combat. Carroll Ishee was openly a combatant, but whether he was also officially a CISPES member is unclear. That CISPES regarded him highly is evident from the dedication in *Reshaping the U.S. Left* which also names Brian Willson and Ben Linder, "who put their lives on the line in the cause of internationalism." This book was edited by Mike Davis and contains a lengthy article by Van Gosse, both of whom were CISPES national staff members at one time or another.

34. Eric Pianin, "U.S. Behind Breakins, Sanctuary Leaders Testify," *The Washington Post*, February 20, 1987, A27.
This is not a direct quotation, but is a reasonable interpretation of Lent's evasive answers when questioned. Lent actually said that FBI Director William Sessions' testimony (that there were links) was "incorrect." When asked directly if CISPES supported the FMLN, Lent evaded the question and (with the assistance of his lawyers) shrilly counter-attacked that the FBI investigation was "illegal." Lent did not answer the question, and his response to it was hardly that of an innocent man.

35. BPR stands for "Bloque Popular Revolucionario", an early "mass" organization fronting for the FPL. It was organized by Commandante "Ana Maria" (Melida Anaya Montes), who was later murdered by order of FPL Commandante General "Marcial."

36. Van Gosse, "The North American Front: Central American Solidarity in the Reagan Era," *Reshaping the U.S. Left: Popular Struggles in the 1980s*, ed. Mike Davis & Michael Sprinkler, (New York: Verso, 1988), 26.

37. House 100-42, 40.

38. Senators William S. Cohen and George J. Mitchell, *Men of Zeal* (New York: Penguin Books, 1988-1989), 2-6.

Chapter 12

# The End of the War

The collapse of the Cold War seriously undercut the rationale behind U.S. policy in El Salvador. An anti-U.S. regime in El Salvador would be a nuisance, but would be unlikely to become a strategic threat. The loss of prestige would be bearable. There was still the possibility of a regional threat developing, but the problem facing the U.S. became thus a largely moral one - having delved so deeply into Salvadoran politics, to abandon El Salvador would be to repeat the 1975 Southeast Asian experience. And then, of course, there were the legal obligations, the 'fig leaf.' The resultant U.S position was summarized by the U.S. Ambassador to the Organization of American States, Luigi Einaudi, in an address to the OAS Permanent Council on February 14, 1991.

> A negotiated political solution and a cease-fire leading to free elections should be at the top of our regional agenda. There has been enough suffering in El Salvador on all sides; the Salvadoran people want peace; they want democracy. All sides need to put maximum efforts to achieve peace in democracy and justice now. The United States commits itself to support these efforts.[1]

## Peace Settlement

In a message dated April 7, 1992, President George Bush officially notified Congress that on January 16, 1992, the Government of El Salvador and representatives of the FMLN had reached a permanent settlement of the conflict, including a final agreement on a ceasefire.[2] Despite all the controversy surrounding it, the policy appears to have succeeded in ending the war in El Salvador without leaving either a left- or right-wing dictatorship in power, and with the human rights situation considerably improved from 1980-1981. But as Benjamin C. Schwartz points out, "a chasm yawns between America's objectives and America's achievements there."[3]

> For a decade, U.S. policy toward El Salvador tried to synthesize liberal and conservative aims: foster political, social, and economic reform, and provide security to a country whose freedom from communism the United States deemed essential. In attempting to reconcile these objectives, however, we pursued a policy by means unsettling to ourselves, for ends humiliating to the Salvadorans, and at a cost disproportionate to any conventional conception of the national interest.[4]

The 'hard-headed realists' who formulated U.S. policy became swept up by their ideals, and instead of a measured response to the Soviet intrusion in Central America, found themselves waging a jumbled crusade against Communist expansion, authoritarian oppression, and social injustice in a country the size of Massachusetts. In retrospect this does not seem to have been the best course of action, but considering the context - the policymakers' perceptions of the situation and what they had to work with - it is understandable. Harsh judgement is easy for critics whose day-to-day decisions don't involve significant risks or responsibilities. The main question left was: What happens now?

## After the War

There seems to have been an idea that the end of the war would usher in a new era of peace and political stability. Experience suggests that this may be something of a vain hope, for several reasons.

1. Violence has been part of Salvadoran political life for a very long time. In 1839-1840 John Lloyd Stephens witnessed a great deal of violence and upheaval as he criss-crossed the already disintegrating Republic of Central America trying to locate a central government to which to present his credentials.[5]

2. Democracy works when a society generally agrees on its principles and aims, and its different political shadings are free to disagree on interpretation of those principles and the proper approach to those aims. As Schwartz notes, such a "social consensus" has still not been reached in El Salvador.[6]

3. The extremists of the right and left have virtually destroyed the political center, making an already polarized political climate even more so.[7] As P.J. O'Rourke rather colorfully described it, being a moderate in El Salvador "is like being in a game of tag where everybody is it but you."[8]

With this in mind it is to be expected that a certain amount of violence will continue, and that there will be more political turbulence in the future. There are some encouraging signs, however. In the March 10, 1991 elections leftist parties "which had no representation in the outgoing congress, made big strides."[9] The Democratic Convergence (CD) won eight seats and the overtly Marxist Nationalist Democratic Union got one. At the May 1, 1991, session of the National Assembly, Ruben Zamora (CD) was elected unanimously to the post of assembly Vice President, voted for by (among others, of course) Roberto D'Aubuisson.[10] President Alfredo Cristiani expressed the hope that the United Nations Truth Commission report, released 15 March 1993, would serve as a "catharsis," since it named human rights violators of both the left and the right.[11] The Salvadoran president also called for a "blanket amnesty" for "anyone who committed a political crime or 'connected common crimes' before Jan. 1, 1992." This amnesty was passed by the National Assembly in what was described as a "stormy legislative session" on 20 March 1993.[12]

On the negative side, the FMLN has complicated the UN Observation Group in El Salvador (ONUSAL) supervised demobilization process by acting in bad faith. It appears to have carefully hoarded its best weapons and personnel.

> The situation has been complicated by the previous demobilization of what was to be the first 20% of the FMLN guerrilla force, but which turned out to be only hundreds of wounded and old veterans with little fighting potential. Their weapons were in no better shape, consisting of rusted and old equipment and not the latest Hungarian and East German AKMs, SA-7s, 14s, 16s, and other Soviet material fielded by the FMLN since 1989.[13]

There have been other maneuvers by the FMLN/FDR, mostly attempts to better its political position without having to meet the demands of the democratic political process. The crime rate is up, with much of it committed by well-armed and organized criminals. There have been accusations that these are demobilized soldiers or guerrillas, and they may indeed be some of both. A particular recent focus of CISPES propaganda has been a series of murders of FMLN leaders, but it is possible that this is not all the work of rightist 'death squads.'

> There is undoubted turmoil within the rank and file of the FMLN; many combatants feel that the Commandancia has abandoned them since the FMLN leaders now live an aristocratic lifestyle. Several former commandants have been gunned down in San Salvador. The FMLN blames resurgent death squads but reliable sources do not discard the possibility that these incidents have been the work of dissatisfied former guerrillas.[14]

Thus it appears that Salvadoran political life will remain livelier and more physically dangerous than U.S. politics. Hopefully, from now on, how the Salvadorans deal with their internal political problems will be for themselves to decide using the fairest means available.

## Notes

1. Luigi R. Einaudi, "Peace and the Consolidation of Democracy in El Salvador," repr. *Dispatch* Vol. 2, No. 8 (February 25, 1991).

2. George Bush, *Assistance for El Salvador*, (Washington DC: Government Printing Office, 1992).

3. Schwartz, 83.

4. Schwartz, 84.

5. John Lloyd Stephens, *Incidents of Travel in Central America, Chiapas and Yucatan*, Vol. 2., (New York: Dover Publications, Inc., 1969), Chap. 3-6.

6. Schwartz, ix.

7. Schwartz, ix.

8. P.J. O'Rourke, *Holidays in Hell*, (New York: Vintage Books. 1988), 137.

9. Associated Press, "Salvador's Rightists Lose Majority, Tally Shows," *The Washington Post*, 24 March 1991, A26.

10. Lee Hockstadter, "Salvadorans Moving to End War," *The Washington Post*, 5 May 1991, A29.

11. Julia Preston, "War Report Names Guilty Salvadorans," *The Washington Post*, 15 March 1993, A13.

12. *The Los Angeles Times*, "Salvadoran Lawmakers Approve Amnesty," *Omaha World-Herald*, 21 March 1993, 15-A.

13. Julio A. Montes, "A New Era in El Salvador," *Jane's Intelligence Review*, January 1993, 47.

14. Montes, 47.

# Conclusion

The war in El Salvador moved into the United States, and was fought there with funding and propaganda between two distinct groups. Official U.S. policy was to support, and assist in the reform of, the elected government of El Salvador. Private proponents of a counter-policy aimed to overthrow that government and help a Marxist minority shoot its way to power. This war of information was for the hearts and minds of the U.S. public and members of the U.S. Congress, and its course certainly affected the course of the war in El Salvador, and may very well have determined the outcome.

# Conclusion

# Appendix

## Present and Former Members of Congress Engaged in Support of the FMLN

All listed are Democrats except Bernie Sanders of Vermont, officially Independent but self-described as a "democratic socialist."

Sister City projects on this list refer to those affiliated with the National Center for U.S.-El Salvador Sister Cities. Despite its name this organization has no connection with Sister Cities International, and its projects were established with illegal, FMLN organized and controlled 'local popular governments' in El Salvador.

Chet Atkins (House-MA) - Sister City
Barbara Boxer (House-CA) - Sister City
George E. Brown (House-CA) - MAES
Benjamin L. Cardin (House-MD) - MAES, Sister City
John Conyers (House-MI) - MAES, NEST
Alan Cranston (Senate-CA) - Sister City
George Crockett (House-MI) - MAES
Tom Daschle (Senate-SD) - Sister City
Dennis DeConcini (Senate-AZ) - Sister City
Ronald Dellums (House-CA) - CISPES, MAES, NEST, SHARE
Julian Dixon (House-CA) - MAES
Mervyn Dymally (House-CA) - CISPES, MAES, NEST
Walter Fauntroy (House-DC) - MAES
Thomas Foglietta (House-PA) - MAES
Robert Garcia (House-NY) - MAES, SHARE
Richard Gephardt (House-MO) - MAES
Tom Harkin (Senate-IA) - MAES
Robert Kastenmeier (House-WI) - Sister City
Edward M. (Teddy) Kennedy (Senate-MA) - SHARE, Sister City
Joseph Kennedy (House-MA) - Sister City
John Kerry (Senate-MA) - MAES, Sister City
Herbert Kohl (Senate-WI) - Sister City

Peter Kostmayer (House-PA) - Sister City
Mickey Leland (House-TX) - MAES
Edward Markey (House-MA) - CISPES, Sister City
Kweisi Mfume (House-MD) - Sister City
Barbara Mikulski (Senate-MD) - CISPES
Parren Mitchell (House-MD) - MAES
Joe Moakley (House-MA) - SHARE, Sister City
Jim Moody (House-TX) - Sister City
James Oberstar (House-MN) - CISPES
Richard Ottinger (House-NY) - MAES
Major Owens (House-NY) - CISPES
Nancy Pelosi (House-CA) - Sister City
Jay Rockefeller (Senate-WV) - MAES
Bernie Sanders (House-VT) - CISPES
Paul Sarbanes (Senate-MD) - Sister City
Patricia Schroeder (House-CO) - CISPES, MAES
Paul Simon (Senate-IL) - MAES
Fortney (Pete) Stark (House-CA) - MAES
Robert Torricelli (House-NY) - CISPES
Bruce F. Vento (House-MN) - MAES
Craig Washington (House-TX) - Sister City
Ted Weiss (House-NY) - CISPES

# Selected Bibliography

Americas Watch. *Violation of Fair Trial Guarantees by the FMLN's Ad Hoc Courts.* New York: Human Rights Watch, 1990.

Blachman, Morris J., William M. LeoGrande and Kenneth E. Sharpe, ed. *Confronting Revolution: Security Through Diplomacy in Central America.* New York: Pantheon Books, 1986.

Bonner, Raymond. *Weakness and Deceit.* New York: Times Books, 1984.

Castellanos, Miguel. *The Commandante Speaks: Memoirs of an El Salvadoran Guerrilla Leader.* Courtney E. Prisk, ed. Boulder, CO: Westview Press, 1991.

Clements, Charles, M.D. *Witness To War.* New York: Bantam Books, 1984.

Collier, Peter & David Horowitz. *Destructive Generation.* New York: Summit Books, 1989.

Cruz, Arturo Jr. *Memoirs of a Counterrevolutionary.* New York: Doubleday, 1989.

Duarte, President Jose Napoleon. *Duarte: My Story.* New York: G.P. Putnam's Sons, 1986.

Fauriol, Georges, ed. *Latin American Insurgencies.* Washington DC: Government Printing Office, 1985.

Gettleman, Marvin E., Patrick Lacefield, Louis Menashe, David Mermelstein and Ronald Radosh, ed. *El Salvador: Central America in the New Cold War.* New York: Grove Press, 1982.

Guevara, Che. *Guerrilla Warfare*, with an introduction and case studies by Brian Loveman and Thomas M. Davies, Jr. New York: Monthly Review Press, 1961; repr. Lincoln NE: University of Nebraska Press, 1985.

Leiken, Robert S., ed. *Central America - Anatomy of Conflict*. New York: Pergamon Press, 1984.

Manwaring, Max G. and Court Prisk, ed. *El Salvador at War*. Washington DC: National Defense University Press, 1988.

McNeil, Frank. *War and Peace in Central America*. New York: Charles Scribner's Sons, 1988.

Musicant, Ivan. *The Banana Wars*. New York: MacMillan Publishing Company, 1990.

Powell, S. Steven. *Covert Cadre: Inside the Institute for Policy Studies*. Ottawa IL: Green Hill Publishers, 1987.

Ra'anan, Uri, Robert L. Pfaltzgraff, Jr., et al. *Hydra of Carnage: International Linkages of Terrorism and Other Low Intensity Operations*. Lexington MA: Lexington Books, 1986.

Radu, Michael, ed. *Violence and the Latin American Revolutionaries*. New Brunswick NJ: Transaction Books, 1988.

Radu, Michael & Vladimir Tismaneanu. *Latin American Revolutionaries: Groups, Goals, Methods*. Washington DC: Pergamon-Brassey's, 1990.

Schwartz, Benjamin C. *American Counterinsurgency Doctrine and El Salvador: The Frustrations of Reform and the Illusions of Nation Building*. Santa Monica CA: RAND, 1991.

Stephens, John L. *Incidents of Travel in Central America, Chiapas and Yucatan*. New York: Dover Books, 1969.

Trager, Oliver, ed. *Latin America: Our Volatile Neighbors*. New York:

Facts On File, 1987.

Waller, J. Michael. *The Third Current of Revolution: Inside the 'North American Front' of El Salvador's Guerrilla War*. Lanham, MD: University Press of America, 1991.

West, Richard. *Hurricane in Nicaragua*. New York: Viking Penguin, 1989.

# Index

Action Networks  77
Agee, Philip  150, 151
Agency for International Development (AID)  132
Agrarian reform
  Land to the Tiller  95
Aid  xiii, 6, 9, 22, 32, 38, 41, 42, 49, 61, 62, 64, 67, 76, 80, 86, 93, 94, 107-113, 117, 130, 131, 145, 148, 149, 151, 161, 165, 166
AK-47  64, 82, 85, 116
AKM
  Eastern bloc  176
Alliance for Progress  42
Americas Watch  xviii, 69, 90, 91, 93, 119, 129, 131, 141, 183
Amnesty International  95
ANDES  18
Angela Sanbrano  61, 79-81, 89, 112
Angola  5, 117
Anthem
  Sandinista  10
Arcatao  113, 116, 161
ARENA  77, 95, 98, 128, 141, 150
Armed Forces of Liberation (FAL)  17
Armed Forces of National Resistance (FARN)  17
Armed Resistance Unit

D.C. bombings  158
arms smuggling  83, 85, 166
Atkins, Chet  179

balance of power  2, 3, 36, 43
  in Realism  2
Berkeley  45, 61, 63, 110, 113
Berryman, Philip  34, 35
Bishop, Maurice  7
bolsones  22
Borge, Tomas  124
Boxer, Barbara  179
BPR  15, 165
Bravo Fund  62, 112, 158, 166
BRAZ  19
brigadistas  117
Brown, George E.  179
Brown, Reverend Gregory S.  86
Bush, George  174

Cabanas  22
Cabezas, Omar  67
Cambridge  61
CAMC  64
Canada  110
'capitalist' weapons  86
Cardin, Benjamin L.  179
Caribbean Basin Initiative  42
Carlos Arias Battalion  19
Carter, Jimmy  33, 46
Casolo, Jennifer Jean  66, 118

Castellanos, Miguel 4, 17, 22, 86, 119
Castro, Fidel 11, 18, 37
  and Angola 7
  on democracy 53
*cayucos* 83
CCR 111
CD 18, 109, 128, 175
ceasefire 174
Center for Constitutional Rights (CCR) 111
Central American Defense Council (CONDECA) 41
Central American Historical Institute 89
Central American Mobilization Coalition (CAMC) 64
Cerron Grande dam 132
Chalatenango 22, 80, 113, 161
Chamorro, Violeta 149
Chandra, Romesh 151
Child, Jack 43
Chinandega, Nicaragua 83
CIA 36, 69, 77, 91, 130, 152, 153, 162
CIAS 111, 115
CISPES 26, 36, 41, 59-64, 66, 69, 78-82, 89, 93, 97, 110-113, 117, 118, 128, 130, 141, 142, 150, 151, 153, 157, 158, 159, 160, 161, 162, 163, 164, 165, 166, 167, 168, 176, 181, 182
  and BPR 166
  as part of FMLN war effort 26
  CPUSA connection 60
  domestic terrorist connections 62
  links with FMLN 166
  membership 61
  relationship with FMLN 61
Clements, Charles 16, 61, 63, 81, 82, 113, 117, 126, 127
COACES 18, 97
coffee xi, 15, 64-67, 97-99, 129-133
COINTELPRO 157
Cold War 7, 33, 38, 45, 173, 183
Collier, Peter 60
Commandancia 176
'Commandante Bravo'
  torture-murder by Sandinistas 51
Committee in Solidarity with the People of El Salvador (see CISPES) 60, 62, 158
Communist Party of El Salvador (PCES) 17
  FAL and UDN 17
Communist Party USA (see CPUSA) 60, 62
Congress xiii, xiv, xv, xxii, 22, 33, 60, 79, 131, 144, 147, 149-152, 162, 164, 166-168, 174, 175, 179, 181
Conservatives (Nicaragua)
  Legitimists 77
Contra/CIA Assassination Manual 69
Contras 96, 110, 111, 162, 163
Conyers, John 152, 153, 161, 181
*Coordinadora* 18
Corr, Edwin G. xiii, 33, 94
Costa Rica ix, 126
Counterpolicy

Principled Realism  53
  revolutionary  51
  U.S. radical left  57
Cranston, Alan  179
Creighton University (Omaha, NE)  65
CRIPDES  115
Cristiani, Alfredo  173
Crockett, George  179
CRM  18
Cruz, Arturo Jr.  10, 53
Cuba  5-7, 16, 22, 24, 36-40, 43, 45, 53, 56, 82, 87, 88, 95, 128, 144
  Guantanamo  38

Dalton, Roque  17, 24, 142
Danceathons  110
Daschle, Tom  179
D'Aubuisson, Roberto  92, 161, 173
Davis, Mike  24, 110, 164, 165
'death squads'  56, 79, 89, 90, 95, 97, 125, 129, 162
Demaziere (Demassiere), Eve  84
Democratic Convergence (CD)  18, 109, 128, 175
Democratic Revolutionary Front (FDR)  18
DeConcini, Dennis  181
Dellums, Ronald  151, 152, 181
  Stockholm Conference on Vietnam  62
DeYoung, Karen  147
DGI (General Directorate of Intelligence)  60
Dissent Memo  82
Dixon, Julian  181

Dodd, Christopher  95, 149
Duarte, Jose Napoleon  35, 36, 130
Duarte Duran, Ines Guadalupe  130

Edwards, Don  152, 153, 161, 165
  and the World Peace Council  152
Einaudi, Luigi  53, 171
El Bloque (Popular Revolutionary Bloc)  17
El Salvador
  government as U.S. puppet  44
  perceptions of war  44
  politics  43
elections  xviii, 33, 34, 53, 55, 79, 126-128, 142, 148, 173, 175
Ellsberg, Daniel  61
EPS 30-11 Battalion
  trained FMLN guerrillas  23
ERP
  Argentine  8
  El Salvador  17
Esquipilas Accords  23
Ethiopia  6, 87

FAL  17-19, 21, 87, 93
FAPU  17, 18
Farabundo Marti, Augustin  14
Farabundo Marti National Liberation Front (see FMLN)  18, 126
FARN  17-19, 21
Farrell, Mike  95
Fauntroy, Walter  181
FBI  60, 62, 64, 80, 111, 113,

150, 153, 157-168
February 28 Popular League (LP-28) 17
Felipe Pena Mendoza Brigade 19
FENASTRAS 69
Filibusters 77
Flores, Luis 62, 158
FMLN xiii, xv, xviii, xxii, 4, 15-27, 35, 36, 40, 41, 43, 44, 53, 55-57, 59-63, 65-69, 77, 78, 80-94, 93, 95, 96, 97, 99, 109-119, 125, 126, 127, 128, 129, 130, 131, 132, 133, 134, 135, 141, 142, 147, 148, 149, 150, 151, 152, 153, 158, 161, 162, 163, 164, 165, 166, 167, 168, 174, 175, 176, 181, 183
   ad hoc courts 129
   and Fidel Castro 18
   and the Black Caucus 151
   and Vietnam 22
   armed propaganda 69
   at war with U.S. 130
   death squads 91
   limited popular support 128
   military organization 18
   news coverage 147
   organization 16
   strategy 24
FMLN 'Final Offensive'
   1982 27
   1989 55
FMLN support network
   Anti-intervention forces 59
   solidarity forces 59
FMLN/FDR
   PCES roots 17
FMSPS 60
FN FAL (assault rifle) 87

foco 24, 39
Foglietta, Thomas 179
Folger's
   coffee boycott of 99
Foreign Agents Registration Act (FARA) 157
Fort Benning 81
'14 Families' 97
FPL 17-19, 21, 25-27, 80, 86, 111, 112, 117, 158, 166
   "Arms for El Salvador" 112
   foreign 'solidarity' groups 26
   protracted war strategy 25
Fronts
   Anastacio Aquino Paracentral 21
   Feliciano Ana Western 21
   Francisco Sanchez Eastern 21
   Metropolitan (San Salvador) 21
   Modesto Ramirez Central 21
   North American (U.S.) 26, 59
FSLN 9, 22, 23
fundraising 61, 63, 79-81, 89, 109, 110, 117, 130, 150, 153

G-3 (assault rifle) 87, 118
Garcia, Napoleon Romero (see also Miguel Castellanos) 119
Garcia, Robert 181
General Command of the FMLN
   Located in Nicaragua 23
Gephardt, Richard 181
Going Home 115
Gosse, Van 26, 36, 37, 51, 59,

67, 80, 166, 167
Grechko, Marshal A. A. 39
Grenada 7, 37
Guazapa 21, 93
*Guerrilla Warfare*
 (Che Guevara) 18
Guevara, Ernesto "Che" 17,
 18, 24, 40, 69, 113
 on mines 133

Handal, Farid 60, 151, 162
 and Dellums 151
Handal, Shafik 86, 110
Harkin, Tom 181
Hernandez Martinez, General
 Maximiliano 16
Hoagland, Peter 64
Honduras ix, 21, 22, 39, 41,
 53, 83, 88, 116
Horowitz, David 62, 183
House of Representatives 80,
 164
 Armed Services Committee
 152, 153
 Intelligence Committee 152
 Subcommittee on Civil and
 Constitutional Rights 18, 111,
 113, 153, 154, 161
 human rights 2, 6, 33, 34, 41,
 43, 51, 52, 54, 56, 65, 68, 81,
 89, 92, 93, 98, 99, 125, 126,
 131, 141, 142, 143, 174, 175,
 183
Hyde, Henry 167

idealism 1, 2, 4, 8, 51, 67,
 135, 168
IFDP 61, 69
Information vigilantes 162
Institute for Food and
 Development Policy (IFDP)
 61
'Insurrectionalism' 27
Inter-American Treaty of
 Reciprocal Assistance (the Rio
 Treaty 40
Intercommunity Center for
 Justice and Peace 69
International Center for
 Development Policy
 Commission on United
 States-Latin American
 Relations 162
International terrorism
 definition 158
IPS 60, 61, 69, 152, 153, 161
Iran xiv, 6, 7, 161, 167
Iran-Contra xiv, 161, 167
Iraq-Gate 168
Ishee, Carroll 63, 117, 163,
 166
Ishee, LaVaun 117

JEWEL 7, 98

Karl, Terry xvii, 109, 127
Kastenmeier, Robert 116, 153,
 161, 181
Kennedy, Edward 182
Kennedy, Joseph 182
Kerry, John 149, 182
KGB 10, 60, 82, 153
Kissinger, Henry 42
Kissinger Commission 42
KKK 162
Kohl, Herbert 182
Kostmayer, Peter 182

La Union 22, 83
Legalism-moralism 2

Leland, Mickey  182
Lent, Michael  26, 79, 111, 166, 167
Letelier, Isabel  60, 161
liberal  xiii, xiv, xv, 8, 60, 68, 77, 143, 149, 164, 174
Liberation Student Movement LSM  117
liberation theology  17, 66
low intensity conflict  xxii, 81
LP-28  17
LPO  17
Luis Adalberto Diaz Battalion  20

Madison, Wisconsin  113, 161
MAES  63, 109, 112, 113, 117, 151, 153, 161, 181, 182
Managua  xiii, 10, 23, 89, 91, 126
Marines  8, 93, 96, 129, 130, 153
Markey, Edward  180
*masas*  109, 111, 115, 116
Mattison, Lindsay  162
Maximiliano Hernandez Brigade  95
Medical Aid For El Salvador (MAES)  63, 151
  aid fraud  112
Mexico  16, 40
Mfume, Kweisi  182
Mikulski, Barbara  182
militia  18, 19, 21
mines  133, 134
Mitchell, Parren  182
Moakley, Joseph  81
Montelimar  85
Moody, Jim  182

Morazan  21, 117
Morgenthau, Hans J.  1
"mortality inflation"  88
MPiKMS-72  20
MPL  17
MPLA  5

N2N  61, 96-99
NACLA  60, 61
National Center for U.S.-El Salvador Sister Cities  181
National Guard
  Nicaragua  8
National interest
  in Realism  2
National Liberation Movement - Tupamaros (MLN)  40
National Republican Alliance (ARENA)  95
Nebraska Peace PAC  64
Nebraskans For Peace  63
negotiations  22, 55, 98
NEST  111, 113, 114, 116, 151, 161, 181
New El Salvador Today (NEST)  113, 151
New Jewel Movement (NJM)  7
New Left  60
New Mobe  63
Newport, Gus  63, 115
Nicaragua  ix, 7-9, 21-23, 35-38, 40, 41, 43, 55, 56, 63, 64, 67-69, 77, 82-84, 86, 87, 89, 96, 117, 126, 143, 149, 152, 158, 162, 185
Nicaragua Medical Aid (NMA)  63
Nicaragua Network  41, 63, 64
Nine Mayors  69, 126

192

NJM 7
Nonalignment 52
'non-military' aid 110
Norton, Chris 69, 142

OAS (Organization of American States) 55, 173
Oberstar, James 182
OCART 64
Omaha Central American Response Team (OCART) 62
Operation Carlota 5
Organization for Liberation from Communism (OLC) 95
Ortega, Daniel 21, 149
Ottinger, Richard 182
Owens, Major 182
Oxfam 83, 84

PAC
 Nebraska Peace 64
PACCA 61, 161
Panama 39, 45
Paraguay 8
Pastors for Peace 69
Pax Christi 56, 64-66, 80, 130
PCES 17, 18, 97
PD-30 33, 34
Pelosi, Nancy 182
Peoples' Revolutionary Army (ERP - 'Montoneros')
 Argentine 8
PFOC 158
Plan Mariposa 86
Plausible deniability
 FMLN aid programs 113
Pledge of Resistance 37, 62-64, 68, 78, 79
PLO 60
Pollack, Sandy 60

Policy Alternatives for the Caribbean and Central America (PACCA) 61, 161
Ponce, Colonel Rene Emilio 55
Popular Liberation Forces (FPL) 80
Popular Liberation Movement (MPL) 17
Popular Revolutionary Bloc (BPR or El Bloque)
 and CISPES 167
 and FPL 17
Popular Workers' League (LPO) 17
PPL 116
*Prairie Fire* 62, 158, 166
Prairie Fire Organizing Committee (PFOC) 158
 and the Weather Underground 62
Principled realism 53
Progressive Hill Staff Group 152
Prolonged popular war 27
propaganda 23, 24, 37, 44, 51, 55, 61, 68, 69, 78, 80, 81, 88, 89, 93, 95, 96, 99, 117-119, 125, 128, 151, 166, 176, 179
PRTC 17-19, 21, 27, 110
Punta Huete Airfield 38

Quest for Peace 79, 115, 116
Quixote Center 56, 65

Radio Venceramos 129
Rafael Aguinada Carranza Battalion 19
Rafael Arce Zablah Brigade

(BRAZ) 19
RAND 43, 184
Reagan, Ronald 42, 150
realism 1, 2, 4, 53, 54, 56, 110
reform x, xxi, 42-44, 56, 69, 97, 98, 174, 179, 184
refugees 113, 115, 116
Regional Coordination for Economic and Social Research (CRIES) 61
repopulation 114-116
Republican 95, 167
revolution x, xviii, 4, 7, 9, 16, 23-25, 35, 39, 40, 44, 53-57, 59, 62, 63, 67, 69, 125, 127, 128, 150, 158, 161, 163, 183, 185
revolutionary 4, 8, 16-19, 24, 25, 37, 40, 51-55, 59-62, 66, 69, 99, 114, 129, 130, 142, 143, 166
Revolutionary Coordination of the Masses (CRM) 18
Revolutionary Party of Central American Workers (PRTC) 17
RN 17, 27
Rockefeller, Jay 182

SA-7 *Strela* missiles 86, 176
SA-14 missiles 23, 176
SA-16 missiles 20, 176
Sacasa, Dr. Juan 8
'Sacred cattle'
 in Congress 150, 164
SALPRESS 117
Samayoa, Salvador 55
San Jorge
 mayors murdered by FMLN 126
Sanbrano, Angela 61, 79-81, 88, 112
sanctuary movement 67
Sanders, Bernie 165, 181, 182
Sandinista
 anti-Americanism 9
 and Fidel Castro 9
 defeat in 1990 elections 148
 Directorate 8
Sandino, Augusto Cesar 8
Sarbanes, Paul 180
School of the Americas (SOA) 81
Schroeder, Patricia 63, 112, 150-153, 182
Schumer, Charles 153, 161
Schwartz, Benjamin C. 43
Secret Anti-Communist Army (ESA) 95
Sensenbrenner, F. James Jr. 161
Sister Cities 113, 116, 181
'Six Jesuits' 65, 69, 78, 81, 119, 148, 150
Slobodin, Alan 166
SOA Watch 81
Socialist Workers Party 62, 135
Somoza, Anastasio 8
Somoza Debayle, Anastasio
 assassination of 8
Soviet
 aerial reconnaissance 38
 bombers 37
 missiles 36
 Navy 38
Soviet Union 2, 4, 6, 10, 36, 37, 39, 40, 44, 53, 55
Stark, Fortney (Pete) 182

194

Students for a Democratic Society 62

Tarver, Rebecca ('Clara') 117, 166
Tequeque 113
Thomas Merton Center 64
Torricelli, Robert 182
Treason 135
Trotskyite 16
Tsetung, Mao 26, 115
Tupamaros 40
Tutela Legal 90, 91, 94, 125

U.S.-El Salvador Institute for Democratic Development 112
Bravo Fund 112
U.S.S.R. 6, 7, 37, 55
UDN 17, 18
Unified Revolutionary Directorate (DRU) 18
United Nations 7, 60, 128, 175
United Popular Action Front (FAPU) 17
United States
as front in Salvadoran civil war 26
University of Nebraska at Omaha 65
UNTS 18, 97
Uruguay 40

Valenzuela, Mauricio
murder by FMLN 126
'Vanguard of the Proletariat' 68
Varelli, Frank 158, 160, 165
Vento, Bruce F. 182
Vietnam x, xii, xiv, 5, 19, 22, 45, 55, 56, 61-64, 78, 87, 96, 133
and FMLN mining campaign 133
vigilante 95, 162
Villalobos, Joaquin 4, 17, 24, 53, 125, 127, 128
execution of Dalton 24
on FMLN terrorism 125
*Violation of Fair Trial Guarantees by the FMLN's Ad Hoc Courts* 129

Walker, William 77
War of the Mayors 125, 141
Washington, Craig 182
Washington Office on Latin America (WOLA) 78
'Weathermen'
Weather Underground Organization (WUO) 62
Weiss, Ted 182
White House 79, 160
White, Robert 162
Witness for Peace 64, 79
WOLA 61, 78

Youth for Peace 63

Zamora, Ruben 175
'Zona Rosa' 65, 69, 96, 128, 129, 131